The Political Economy of Trade Integration

Contributions to Economics

Peter R. Haiss
Cultural Influences on Strategic Planning
1990. ISBN 3-7908-0481-9

Manfred Kremer/Marion Weber (Eds.)
Transforming Economic Systems: The Case of Poland
1992. ISBN 3-7908-0585-8

Marcel F. van Marion
Liberal Trade and Japan
1993. ISBN 3-7908-0699-4

Hans Schneeweiß/
Klaus F. Zimmermann (Eds.)
Studies in Applied Econometrics
1993. ISBN 3-7908-0716-8

Gerhard Gehrig/
Wladyslaw Welfe (Eds.)
Economies in Transition
1993. ISBN 3-7908-0721-4

Christoph M. Schneider
Research and Development Management: From the Soviet Union to Russia
1994. ISBN 3-7908-0757-5

Bernhard Böhm/
Lionello F. Punzo (Eds.)
Economic Performance
1994. ISBN 3-7908-0811-3

Michael Reiter
The Dynamics of Business Cycles
1995. ISBN 3-7908-0823-7

Michael Carlberg
Sustainability and Optimality of Public Debt
1995. ISBN 3-7908-0834-2

Lars Olof Persson/Ulf Wiberg
Microregional Fragmentation
1995. ISBN 3-7908-0855-5

Andreas Foerster
Institutional Analysis of Development Administration
1995. ISBN 3-7908-0853-9

Ernesto Felli/Furio C. Rosati/
Giovanni Tria (Eds.)
The Service Sector: Productivity and Growth
1995. ISBN 3-7908-0875-X

Giuseppe Munda
Multicriteria Evaluation in Fuzzy Environment
1995. ISBN 3-7908-0892-X

Boris Maurer
R & D, Innovation and Industrial Structure
1996. ISBN 3-7908-0900-4

Giovanni Galizzi/Luciano Venturini (Eds.)
Economics of Innovation: The Case of Food Industry
1996. ISBN 3-7908-0911-X

David T. Johnson
Poverty, Inequality and Social Welfare in Australia
1996. ISBN 3-7908-0942-X

Rongxing Guo
Border-Regional Economics
1996. ISBN 3-7908-0943-8

Oliver Fratzscher

The Political Economy of Trade Integration

With 10 Figures

Physica-Verlag
A Springer-Verlag Company

Series Editors
Werner A. Müller
Peter Schuster

Author
Dr. Oliver Fratzscher
International Monetary Fund
700 19th Street, N.W.
Washington, DC 20431
USA

The views expressed are those of the author and should not be attributed to the International Monetary Fund.

Die Deutsche Bibliothek – CIP-Einheitsaufnahme
Fratzscher, Oliver:
The political economy of trade integration/Oliver Fratzscher. – Heidelberg: Physica-Verl., 1996
(Contribution to economics)
ISBN-13: 978-3-7908-0945-9 e-ISBN-13: 978-3-642-61490-3
DOI: 10.107/978-3-642-61490-3

Softcover reprint of the hardcover 1st edition 1996

SPIN 10538445 88/2202-5 4 3 2 1 0 – Printed on acid-free paper

For My Parents

With Gratitude

PREFACE

This dissertation looks at increasing trade integration from three angles: First, what are welfare implications of trade integration and trading blocks? Second, what mechanism can improve the sustainability of trade integration? Third, what relationship evolved between trade and foreign direct investment?

Chapter I starts by questioning Krugman's (1993) trading block model, which suggested that world trade is increasingly conducted between three trading blocks, which produces a minimum in world welfare. His symmetrical trading block model is extended into a two-sector model, where trade is not only beneficial through increased varieties in a Dixit-Stiglitz framework, but also through comparative advantage. Results show that:

(i) regionalism and multilateralism can be compatible and welfare enhancing;

(ii) sequential integration can monotonously increase world welfare;

(iii) more dissimilar countries have higher potential benefits from integration;

(iv) about one third of potential gains from free-trade under average tariffs are already realized in a system of three trading blocks.

Chapter II studies the political sustainability of trade integration. The previous trading-block-model is combined with a political pressure group model, where domestic interest groups lobby their government to proceed with sequential trade integration. Theory shows that trade integration is politically not sustainable when consumers' and producers' interests are opposed, unless a mechanism is designed which links sequential trade integration with factor reallocation and which worsens the best alternative to integration. An application to the case of Central European integration shows that such a mechanism has been implemented, but that special interests in the European Union oppose new memberships.

Chapter III asks whether foreign direct investment (FDI) is a substitute or complement for international trade, since both possibilities are modelled in the theory of multinational firms. A gravity model estimates the cumulative effect for a sample of 63 countries and suggests that FDI inflows *reduce* overall trade and in some cases deteriorate the trade balance. Three channels are identified in case studies of Spain, Mexico, and Thailand but need to be quantified in further research. Predictions should not be based on the gravity model because it appears structurally unstable.

As a result, some policy implications are also reflected from three angles:

· First, regional integration (for example NAFTA, APEC, ASEAN, CEFTA, EU) as a parallel process to multilateral integration (within the WTO) is usually welfare enhancing, and most squabbles are about redistribution.

· Second, redistribution appears as a key obstacle to integrating Central Europe into the European Union, which requires a mechanism to improve the political sustainability by reallocating factors away from agriculture, by strengthening multi-nationals as key proponents, by allocating structural funds to disadvantaged regions, and by worsening any alternative to integration.

· Third, trade integration often coincides with increasing flows of FDI, which can have various macro-economic effects: a direct effect of FDI inflows usually substitutes for trade, an indirect effect usually increases investment and thereby complements trade, and an exchange rate effect can deteriorate the trade balance.

Completing this dissertation has been a great intellectual and personal challenge, and I am deeply grateful for the support I received from my advisors, colleagues, friends, and sponsors. I could not have succeeded without the great enthusiasm of my parents and my teachers in Germany and in Canada, especially of Professor Ulrich Blum and Professor Leonard Dudley. I was then extremely fortunate to be guided by Professor Dale Jorgenson as my mentor at Harvard, and by the invaluable support of my advisors, Professor Robert Lawrence and Professor Shang-Jin Wei. Many ideas were generated during my work for the Polish Council of Ministers in 1992-93, with special thanks to then deputy prime minister Jan-Krzysztof Bielecki and to Professor Jeffrey Sachs, whereas most theoretical work was completed while I was visiting the Brookings Institution during 1993-94 where I was most grateful for the support of Dr. Barry Bosworth.

Moreover, I could not have completed this dissertation in such a focused and timely fashion without the various financial support, especially the generous grants from Harvard University and the Gottlieb-Daimler and Karl-Benz Foundation through the National Science Foundation, and the scholarships from the Colonia-Foundation, the German Academic Exchange Service (DAAD), and the Konrad-Adenauer Foundation. Finally, one very special appreciation should go to my wife Jianping for her endless support, love and encouragement.

Oliver Fratzscher

Washington D.C.
in March 1996

Contents

INDEX OF TABLES AND FIGURES

Regionalism and Multilateralism: How Are They Compatible ?

-- A Symmetrical Two-Sector Trading Block Model

Abstract:

Chapter I studies trade and welfare effects from regional integration. World trade is increasingly conducted between three trading blocks, but world welfare has not declined, as predicted by Krugman. His symmetrical trading block model is extended into a two-sector-model, where trade is beneficial through increased varieties and comparative advantage. Simulations confirm that:

(i) regionalism and multilateralism can be compatible and welfare enhancing;

(ii) sequential integration can monotonously increase world welfare;

(iii) more dissimilar countries have higher potential benefits from integration;

(iv) about one third of potential gains from free-trade under average tariffs are already realized in a system of three trading blocks.

Keywords: trading block; monopolistic competition; comparative advantage; bilateralism; multilateralism; regionalism; economic integration.

1. INTRODUCTION

Regionalism is spreading like wildfire, as Richard Baldwin (1993) recently remarked: The European Union continues to expand towards Scandinavia and Central Europe, the North American Free Trade Agreement might soon expand towards Southern America, and Asian nations are more serious than ever to advance ASEAN as a third regional trading block. Already today, more than 94% of world trade is conducted within or between these three giant trading blocks. Meanwhile, after the conclusion of multilateral trade negotiations of the Uruguay Round in 1993, barriers to trade have continued to decline, and regional blocks seem to become more integrated in the world economy.

But how beneficial is that phenomenon we call wildfire? There are some political considerations in favor of trading blocks, such as migration and security concerns. On the other hand, economists tend to evaluate trading regimes according to their overall economic benefits. This paper studies primarily the economic impact of an increasing regionalization of world trade on overall world welfare, while political and distributional issues are only briefly mentioned. At the outset, we start by analyzing the theoretical and empirical validity of Krugman's (1993) influential trading block model, which suggested that a structure of three trading blocks implies the worst possible outcome on world welfare. Krugman developed a fully symmetric model and argued that high protectionist tariffs become most distortionary if applied by players with large market power, and that benefits from integration arise only after the point where three trading blocks integrate to one block, which is called free trade.

This paper presents a trading block model which extends Krugman's one-sector framework by modelling two sectors with comparative advantage in a symmetric world, where trade is beneficial through increased varieties and specialization. Our first question asks about the impact of regional integration on world welfare, and it is demonstrated that within a realistic range of parameters, every step of increasing regional integration is improving world welfare. We also show that in a world with comparative advantage and average tariffs, one third of the potential benefits from free trade are already realized under a structure of three trading blocks. These results advocate that regionalism and multilateralism are not exclusive, but they can be compatible with each other, and they both can improve world welfare.

The second question of this paper then, as revealed in the title, asks how these two regimes are compatible, how regionalism can be most beneficial, and more specifically, whether integration of similar or dissimilar countries is preferable. We have recently witnessed the integration of rather dissimilar countries in terms of size and GDP per capita, with the Southern European countries joining the European Community in the 1980s and with Mexico joining the North American Free Trade Agreement in 1993. On the basis of a fully symmetric model, our analysis shows that integration among dissimilar countries can increase world welfare by up to 30%. Moreover, some areas for further research on political economy and distributional issues are identified, which could extend our symmetric and static model to a more complete framework for the study of trade and welfare effects in our more complex trading block regime.

The following part starts answering the first question with a brief reality check, reviewing whether world trade has become more regionalized and how world welfare has been affected. Drawing on trade data from recent empirical studies, we find that in some areas world trade has become more regionalized. However, the overall trade volume for both intra- and extra-regional trade has grown faster than overall GDP since 1948, which implies that world welfare has increased. In contrast, Krugman's trading block model, which is presented in part 3, comes to the conclusion that the current structure of three trading blocks minimizes world welfare, but it seems that his assumptions of no comparative advantage and optimal tariffs drive that result. In order to answer our two main questions from a more solid theoretical perspective, we develop a similar trading block model in part 4, which is based on a two-sector model introducing comparative advantage and on tariffs set exogenously. It illustrates that for a wide range of parameters, world welfare rises monotonously with increasing regionalization. That finding is strengthened by the introduction of inter-continental transport costs and the possibility that some trade barriers remain within trading blocks. In a final part, the conclusions and ideas for further research are summarized.

2. A LOOK AT TRADE DATA: MORE REGIONALISM AND MORE WELFARE

This part answers the first question by reviewing the theoretical relationship between regional integration and world welfare, and then by analyzing empirically whether and how world trade has become more regionalized. We follow the hypothesis by Kemp and Wan (1976) that trade volumes rather than trade shares better predict world welfare, which suggests that expanding intra- and extra-regional trade volumes since 1948 have improved welfare. We also present two relative indicators showing that trade has become more regionalized in some regions.

Starting with a note on nomenclature, theorists use the term *regional integration agreements* (RIAs) as a general term for a variety of structures[1/]. More recently, a similarly general term *regional trading block* has been used to describe the importance of trade in RIAs. However, regional trading blocks refer to very different structures across regions, ranging from a preferential trade agreement in Asia, to NAFTA in America and an Economic Union in Europe.

1/ We distinguish *preferential trade agreements* (PTAs, in which signatories impose reduced tariffs on each other's imports), *free trade areas* (FTAs, in which tariffs are eliminated on nearly all imports from member states), *customs unions* (CUs, which also introduce a common external tariff of all member states), *common markets* (CMs, which also allow the free movement of factors among member states), and *economic unions* (EUs, which involve a wider harmonization of policies).

Moreover, the term *regionalism* indicates that regional trade has become more important. However, the causes of that effect may be natural or policy factors, as for instance strong economic growth in Asia compared to specific regional trade policies in Europe.

Trade and welfare effects of regional integration agreements have been one of the widely discussed issues among trade theorists in the post-war years, starting from the seminal work of Viner (1950), to Meade (1955), Lipsey (1957), and more recently Wooton (1986), Wonnacott and Lutz (1989), and Baldwin (1989). These studies concluded that free trade between all countries is a pareto-optimal allocation in a competitive world. However, they also recognized political and institutional factors that hinder free trade. Srinivasan, Whalley, and Wooton (1993) pointed out that a small-open country may increase its national welfare by imposing a small tariff, although it is a second-best solution for world welfare. Two important concepts have been developed to study the relationship between regional integration and world welfare:

Jacob Viner (1950) distinguished two welfare effects which evolve from regional rather than multilateral integration: *Trade creation* occurs when domestic products are substituted by lower-cost imports from a partner-country, while *trade diversion* occurs when least-expensive imports from outside countries are substituted by more expensive imports from partner-countries. Although these categories are useful for descriptive purposes, they prove inappropriate for measuring welfare effects. Viner assumed that in general, trade creation is welfare enhancing and trade diversion is welfare reducing, but there are important exceptions: Meade (1955) and Lipsey (1957) pointed out that under trade diversion, prices may be lower because of reduced tariffs, which leads to less distortion in consumption, and hence higher welfare. Wonnacott and Lutz (1989) explained that improved economies of scale and rising non-tariff barriers make it even more difficult to derive clear welfare implications from these *relative* measures.

Kemp and Wan (1976) focused on another concept linking the *absolute volume* of a intra- and extra-regional trade to world welfare. They argued that incentives for exporters must be sufficiently large to allow a government to proceed to liberalization despite the losses incurred by import substituting industries, and that liberalization typically requires internal as well as international transfers which are much easier to agree upon in a regional rather than multilateral agreement. They demonstrated that, while maintaining the same *volume (not share)* of trade with the rest of the world, any group of countries could benefit from internal trade liberalization. Consequently, constant extra-regional trade and increased intra-regional trade *can* improve world welfare, but the result crucially depends on the characteristics and implementation of any RIA. Moreover, they illustrated that increasing regionalism *can* improve world welfare, since any move from a RIA of n countries to a RIA of (n+1) countries can be structured as an improvement of pareto-efficiency. Wooton (1986) confirmed these insights with an elaborated model and concluded that the observation of world trade becoming more regional (as a ratio of intra- to extra-regional trade) need not indicate any harm to world welfare.

There have been many more sophisticated arguments linking regional integration and world welfare. The most important one has been presented by Bhagwati (1992), suggesting that world welfare could have been higher in the absence of RIAs if all liberalization had been multilateral. However, that counter-factual argument is impossible to prove and even the hypothesis that all RIAs could be achieved on a multilateral basis is hard to sustain in an environment where domestic political economy issues are essential. Baldwin (1989) added another dimension arguing that RIAs can create additional growth effects which improve welfare.

For our purpose, we stay with Kemp and Wan's hypothesis that an increased volume of intra- (extra-) regional trade improves regional (world) welfare. We now first study data on absolute trade volumes, which show that world welfare has improved, and we then study data on relative regional trade shares, which show that world trade has become more regionalized in some areas. Table 1 gives a first impression on the growth of absolute world trade over the course of a century. It indicates that world merchandise exports have grown faster than world GDP in all periods since 1870, except for the inter-war period from 1913-1950, which was characterized by a devastating depression and disintegration. The most remarkable growth of exports has occurred since 1950, which coincided with both multilateral and regional integration:

Table 1: Annual Percentage Growth in World GDP and World Merchandise Exports

	1870 to 1900	1900 to 1913	1913 to 1950	1950 to 1973	1973 to 1987
World GDP	2.9	2.5	2.0	4.8	3.3
Merch. Exports	3.8	4.3	0.6	7.6	4.5

Data: adapted from Blackhurst and Henderson (1993).
Note: World indices include 14 largest economies for the period 1870-1900 and 32 largest economies for all other periods.

Several rounds of *multilateral trade agreements* based on the most-favored nation clause (MFN) have been implemented. The principle of nondiscrimination of the MFN-clause created global order out of an essentially mercantilist system and tariffs were substantially reduced[2/], averaging in 1987 on the eve of the Uruguay round 4.9% for the United States, 6.0% for the European Community, and 6.0% for Japan. However, the character of protection changed from tariffs into a system of voluntary export restraints, anti-dumping mechanisms, and other non-tariff barriers in different institutional settings. Table 2 shows estimates for combined tariff- and non-tariff-barriers for trade among the three trading blocks, where the average ad valorem rate of protection is in the range of 15% to 20% (henceforth referred to as *average tariff*).

2/ De Melo and Panagariya (1993) quote the US tariff as an example, which at the conclusion of the Tokyo round in 1979 had declined by more than 90% since the first round of multilateral talks started in Geneva in 1947.

Table 2: Ad Valorem Average Rates of Protection by Region (1986)

Destination → ↓ Origin	United States	Canada	European Union	Rest of Europe	Japan
United States	--	9.4	19.8	13.1	22.7
Canada	8.2	--	19.1	14.3	23.5
EuropeanUnion	12.3	12.7	--	6.9	15.3
Rest of Europe	11.4	12.7	10.1	--	13.1
Japan	9.3	10.5	18.3	10.3	--

Data: adapted from Perroni and Whalley (1994).
Note: Ad valorem estimates combine tariff and non-tariff rates and include protection effects of domestic agricultural programs, textile quotas, restrictions in services, and other VERs.

Expanding trade resulted both from *natural effects*, such as reduced international transport costs and increasing specialization leading to more intra-industry trade, and from *policy effects*, such as multilateral reductions in tariffs and regional trading arrangements. Since 1948, the share of world GDP traded increased from 22% to 35%, with the European economies trading 45% of their GDP, Asia 29%, and America 20%. As revealed in table 2, the percentage share of world trade in 1990 declined to 20% for America, increased to 21% for Asia, and to 51% for Europe. However, that does in no case imply that trade volumes declined, rather that growth in Asia and Europe has been larger than growth in American trade.

Besides progress in multilateral trade liberalization, we also witnessed two waves of *regional trading arrangements* after the second world war. The first wave occurred during the 1960s and spread under the impetus of the European

Common Market throughout Africa, Latin America, and other developing countries, but finally came to a halt in the 1970s. The second period which started in the middle of the 1980s seems to remain more permanent. The United States, previously a strong supporter of multilateralism, formed a free-trade-agreement with Canada and Mexico, and at the same time European integration spread with the Southern enlargement and the cooperation agreements with EFTA and Central European countries. Moreover, old arrangements have been revived throughout Africa, Asia, Latin America, and the Middle East, and also some new regional arrangements evolved.

Now we turn our analysis to developments in intra- and extra-regional trade as *shares* of GDP, and we see in table 3 that both shares were around 17% as a world average in 1990, but with a tendency for intra-regional trade as a share of GDP to rise especially in Europe. Although most studies confirm that impression, these indicators are substantially biased: First, the breakdown of colonial ties in the 1950s and 1960s explain the decreasing European share of extra-regional trade (which did not necessarily decrease world welfare). Second, increasing oil-prices in the 1980s explain that extra-regional trade shares for the world stagnated during that period (which usually is assumed to have decreased world welfare). Third, by enlarging trading blocks for instance with the Southern European integration, formerly extra-regional trade becomes inter-regional (purely a change in accounting). And finally, data in table 3 only account for merchandise trade, while trade in agriculture, especially in the European Union, is supposedly more intra-regional, whereas trade in services has recently become more extra-regional. Hence it is indeed very difficult to draw any implication from trade shares to welfare.

Anderson and Norheim (1993) proposed an improved indicator to measure intra- and extra-regional trade, which normalizes both for GDP growth and for growth of world trade and also accounts for changes in the definition of regions. As shown in equation (1), the propensity to trade intra- (extra-) regionally is defined as the intra- (extra-) regional trade as share of GDP (nominator) over the openness of the trading-partner-region (denominator). The lower part of table 3 indicates that the propensities to trade both intra- and extra-regionally have in general increased since 1948, with the exception of Europe, where the extra-regional indicator declined especially in the 1980s, while the intra-regional one increased especially in the 1970s.

$$I_{ij} = \frac{X_{ij} * R_i}{M_j}$$

$$\begin{aligned} I_{ij} &= \textit{Propensity of Exports } (i \to j) \\ X_{ij} &= \textit{Exports}(i \to j) \;/\; \textit{Total Exports}(i) \\ R_i &= \textit{Total Exports}(i) \;/\; \textit{GDP}(i) \\ M_j &= \textit{Imports}(j) \;/\; \textit{World Imports}(k \neq j) \end{aligned} \qquad (1)$$

Table 3: Indices of Intra-/Extra-regional World Merchandise Trade

	1928	1938	1948	1958	1968	1979	1990
Share of GDP traded (%)							
Europe	33.1	24.1	33.6	31.5	34.8	46.2	45.4
America	13.9	10.2	13.9	11.8	10.9	20.9	20.4
Asia	31.9	24.1	24.6	26.3	21.2	27.3	29.2
World	24.3	19.8	22.4	21.7	21.8	34.6	33.5
Share of World Trade (%)							
Europe	51.8	51.2	41.7	48.8	53.3	51.4	51.2
America	26.3	22.4	33.9	27.9	24.2	20.8	20.5
Asia	18.0	14.6	14.6	13.5	13.3	15.3	21.4
Intra-Regional Trade as share of GDP (%)							
Europe	20.1	14.6	17.2	19.1	24.5	33.4	34.3
America	6.2	4.4	7.9	6.6	5.7	9.7	9.2
Asia	14.5	16.0	9.6	10.8	7.8	11.2	14.0
World	9.4	7.4	7.3	8.8	10.3	15.9	17.4
Extra-Regional Trade as share of GDP (%)							
Europe	13.0	9.5	16.5	12.4	10.2	12.8	11.1
America	7.7	5.9	6.0	5.2	5.2	11.2	11.2
Asia	17.4	8.1	15.1	15.5	13.5	16.1	15.2
World	14.9	12.4	14.9	12.9	11.6	18.8	16.1
Propensity to trade intra-regionally							
Europe	0.40	0.29	0.42	0.40	0.47	0.66	0.68
America	0.25	0.20	0.25	0.24	0.24	0.48	0.46
Asia	0.83	0.76	0.67	0.83	0.60	0.76	0.67
World	0.45	0.37	0.54	0.57	0.61	0.91	0.88
Propensity to trade extra-regionally							
Europe	0.26	0.19	0.27	0.24	0.21	0.26	0.22
America	0.10	0.07	0.08	0.07	0.07	0.14	0.14
Asia	0.21	0.16	0.18	0.18	0.15	0.19	0.19
World	0.21	0.16	0.19	0.16	0.15	0.23	0.21

Data: adapted from Anderson and Blackhurst (1993) and Anderson and Norheim (1993).
Note: World indices are calculated as weighted averages of regions.

Resuming, world trade since 1948 has grown much faster than world GDP, pushed both by natural and policy effects. World trade has become more regionalized especially in Europe, but this has not precluded ongoing integration of the global economy, and it appears that it has not been welfare reducing. Srinivasan, Whalley and Wooton (1993) surveyed a variety of studies which confirmed that regional integration has produced small but positive welfare effects. However, the question whether world welfare would have grown faster without regionalization remains open, with Bhagwati (1992) arguing that regional arrangements were stumbling blocks which hindered further multilateral arrangements, and Lawrence (1991) arguing that regional arrangements were building blocks which supported multilateral agreements since they have become more inclusive, and they also improved credibility and governance.

3. KRUGMAN'S TRADING BLOCK MODEL

Paul Krugman (1991a and 1991b) suggested that the overall effect from changes in the world trading system on world welfare depends on the actual extent of regionalization, which he measured as the size of trading blocks. In his ingenious model, world welfare is a V-shaped function: world welfare is maximized under free trade and minimized under three trading blocks, and then monotonously rising when the world becomes less regionalized. Apparently, today's trading structure is characterized by three main trading blocks, and it is surprising that this should be the worst situation for world welfare. Since that view is also contrary to the widely held intuition which emerged after the arguments presented in the previous part, Krugman's trading block model became the focus for a controversial debate. In the following part, Krugman's trading block model is briefly presented and then discussed, before a two-sector-model introducing comparative advantage will be developed in the subsequent part.

We only recapitulate the basic features of Krugman's (1991a) model, which we simplify in some areas for reasons of exposition. The basic model was developed as a trade model under monopolistic competition by Krugman (1980), based on the Dixit-Stiglitz framework (1977). The market structure is the type of Chamberlinian monopolistic competition, and *trade is only driven by the taste for a variety of differentiated products*. This is the opposite case to Ricardo's traditional model[3/] where trade developed because of comparative advantage and countries specializing in different industries.

Krugman's differentiated products world consists of a large number of countries N, which are grouped into a number of symmetric trading blocks C, each consisting of N/C countries. Each country has only one industry, with the same technology in production and the same tastes of consumers. In this simplified world, the question of regionalism is reduced to the following: How does world welfare depend on the number of trading blocks C?

3/ The traditional reference is David Ricardo's (1817) book, where he explained trade between Portugal and England which led these countries to specialize in different products.

Each country produces only differentiated products, which are unique and hence imperfect substitutes for each other and for products of other countries. All goods enter symmetrically into the demand function, with a constant elasticity of substitution between any pair of goods. Therefore, every consumer in the world has tastes represented by the CES utility function (2), where i indices the various goods, n indicates the total number of goods being produced, and the parameter $\Theta \in (0,1)$ indicates the taste for variety, ranging from extreme ($\Theta=0$) to indifferent ($\Theta=1$).

$$U = \sum_{i=1}^{n} (c_i)^{\theta} \quad with\ 0<\theta<1 \tag{2}$$

Labor is the only factor of production and it is completely immobile. Increasing returns are introduced by assuming a fixed cost in addition to a constant marginal cost of production. The cost function (3) is common to all varieties, where labor market equilibrium implies (4):

$$l_i = \alpha + \beta * x_i \quad with\ \alpha,\beta>0 \tag{3}$$

$$L = \sum_{i=1}^{n} l_i = \sum_{i=1}^{n} (\alpha + \beta * x_i) \tag{4}$$

In a *closed economy*, the equilibrium is determined by first deriving the inverse demand function (6) from the maximization problem of a consumer (5), then by deriving the equilibrium price (8) from the profit maximization of the firm (7), and finally by deriving the equilibrium output (9) from the zero-profit condition. It should be recalled that under Chamberlinian monopolistic competition, each firm has some monopoly power which is used to mark-up prices, but profits are driven to zero by the free entry and exit conditions.

$$Max\ U = \sum_{i=1}^{n} (c_i)^{\theta} \quad s.t. \quad w - \sum_{i=1}^{n} (c_i * p_i) \geq 0 \tag{5}$$

$$p_i = \frac{\theta * (x_i / L)^{\theta - 1}}{\lambda} \tag{6}$$

$$Max\ \pi_i = p_i * x_i - (\alpha + \beta * x_i) * w \quad with\ \epsilon_i = \frac{1}{1-\theta} \tag{7}$$

$$p_{i_{equil}} = \frac{\beta * w}{\theta} \tag{8}$$

$$\begin{aligned} &\pi_i = p * x_i - (\alpha + \beta * x_i) * w = 0 \\ \Leftrightarrow \quad & x_{i_{equil}} = \frac{\alpha * \theta}{\beta * (1 - \theta)} \end{aligned} \tag{9}$$

Given equilibrium prices and output, the labor market equilibrium (4) determines the equilibrium number of varieties n, as expressed in equation (10). Once we determined these equilibrium values, we can go back to the consumer's budget constraint (5) and calculate the equilibrium consumption of each product, which then determines the consumer's utility (2).

$$n_{equil} = \frac{L * (1 - \theta)}{\alpha} \tag{10}$$

In an *open economy*, consumers can buy home and foreign products. Tariffs introduce a relatively larger demand for home products than for foreign products, that ratio is called σ.

$$\sigma_t = \frac{c_{i_{foreign}}}{c_{i_{home}}} = \left(\frac{p}{p_t}\right)^{\frac{1}{1-\theta}} = (1+t)^{\frac{1}{(\theta-1)}} < 1 \tag{11}$$

Consumers then spend a share SH=(N/C)/{N/C+σ*(N-N/C)} on products from home countries, and a share SF={σ*(N-N/C)}/{N/C+σ*(N-N/C)} on products from foreign countries. In that open economy, consumers can exchange one green apple from home production for σ red apples from foreign production, and depending on their taste for variety Θ, they may increase their overall utility. However, it should be noted that in this simple open economy model, there are no changes in prices (p), quantities (x), and varieties (n) from the closed economy version; as indicated in equations (8) through (10), these variables only depend on parameters.

Krugman assumes that blocs set tariffs as in equation (12) which maximize their welfare, taking policies of other trading blocks as given. The tariff revenue is then redistributed equally to home consumers, but they have a distortionary impact on relative demands σ.

$$t_{opt} = \frac{1}{(1-s)*(\sigma-1)} \quad with\ \sigma = \frac{1}{1-\theta} \quad and \quad s = [(1+t)^{\sigma}+C-1]^{-1} \tag{12}$$

From a similar consumer budget constraint as (5), where wages and tariff redistribution equal expenditure on home and foreign products, we can now determine the equilibrium consumption of each home and foreign product, which only depends on parameter C, the number of trading blocks. When these consumption formulae are replaced into the utility function (2), we receive the desired relationship of utility depending only on the number of trading blocks.

At one extreme (C=N), with as many blocks as countries, each block is too small to have any market power. Therefore, optimal tariffs are close to zero and competitive behavior maximizes world welfare, with only small distortions. At the other extreme (C=1), with only one trading block, there is no tariff at all since this is a perfect world of free trade. Here, world welfare is maximized, a value which we normalize to one. In between, welfare reaches a minimum where the distortionary effects of tariffs are largest, which for Krugman's parameters turns out to be at C=3. This result is robust to alternative tariff-formation processes, as it is illustrated in figure 3, where tariffs are set exogenously at t=0.25 and the parameter Θ ranges from 0.7 to 0.8. A higher taste for variety (lower Θ) implies a lower world welfare in autonomy, since the reduction in world trade becomes more costly in terms of utility.

Krugman's model has been very successful in reviving a controversial debate, it certainly is a little simplistic, but developed in an ingenious way, producing very surprising results. Srinivasan commented that it *"comes uncomfortably close to being theory without relevance"* (1993, page 85), and more specifically, it has been criticized from four perspectives, although no good alternative model has yet been developed:

First, Srinivasan (1993) and Deardorff and Stern (1992) argued that one key assumption of the model clearly stacks the cards against bilateralism, namely the framework of differentiated products. Within a single-sector monopolistic-competition model, each country's products are imperfect substitutes for those of all other countries, something similar to the Armington assumption, which assigns a great importance to imports of other countries' unique products. When countries form trading blocks, trade with outside countries is diverted towards trade within the block. The effects of this trade diversion on welfare are strongly exaggerated in Krugman's model, since the loss of variety is very costly in an environment of differentiated products.

Second, Krugman's model also significantly underestimates the extent of trade creation. Since all countries have identical production functions, there can be no benefits from trade through comparative advantage. The intuition that trade creation is larger among countries with significant comparative advantage was recently formulated in a model by Srinivasan (1993): Suppose that labor as the only factor of production can produce two goods, and that half of the countries have comparative advantage in the first good, and the other half in the second good. If we now divide the world into two blocs each consisting of identical countries, welfare will be below the maximum level. However, if we divide the world into two identical blocks each consisting of one half of countries of each type, welfare will be at its maximum level, coinciding with the level achieved under free trade. A disadvantage of that model, however, is that countries are no longer fully symmetric and hence there is no longer a constant relationship between the number of trading blocks and world welfare.

Resuming the first two lines of criticism, the structure of complete product differentiation without allowing for any comparative advantage implies an overestimation of trade diversion and an underestimation of trade creation, and therefore biases the outcome against regionalism. Moreover, the unrealistic assumption of optimal tariffs reinforces the overestimation of trade diversion occurring after the formation of trading blocks, since larger trading blocks with more market power imply higher optimal tariffs and hence larger distortionary effects. For example, in the case of two trading blocks the level of optimal tariffs under Krugman's parameters is around 75%, for three trading blocks it is around 55%[4/], values which are much higher than today's actual ad valorem tariffs which we presented in table 2 of the previous part.

4/ Unfortunately, Krugman (1991a and 1991b) did not provide the exact values for optimal tariffs. Haveman (1993, figure 2) calculated average rates of the optimal tariff under a variety of parameters, which are much larger than any empirical observation.

The third line of criticism was voiced by Srinivasan (1993), arguing that the real world is one of heterogeneity and asymmetry (1993, page 88). While the previous criticism could possibly be incorporated into Krugman's model, this line of criticism is not as helpful since the ingenuity of Krugman's model comes from his ability to solve a complex trading block model by assuming full symmetry across countries. Deardorff and Stern (1992) followed that idea, simplified the framework by dropping the production side, then defined asymmetric endowments of products across countries, and studied for some special cases the sequential formation of one trading block which is growing by including single isolated outside countries. However, that approach not only appears less realistic in assuming only one expanding trading block, but it also complicates the relationship between the size of that trading block and the level of world welfare. Haveman (1993) actually developed a full-scale stochastic model, running a large number of random experiments choosing different types of countries as members of that trading block, and then calculated average values for world welfare for different block sizes. Although his results seem to confirm Krugman's intuition, the huge size of the variances make his conclusions much less credible.

Finally, a fourth line of criticism distinguishes between Krugman's comparative-static approach and the dynamic time-path implications, which illuminate the political economy of trading block formation and ask whether regionalism helps or hurts the eventual evolution of worldwide free trade. Opinions among economists on that question are also controversial: Lawrence

(1991) and Summers (1991) argued that regionalism helps to move the world along to free trade since it reduces the number of negotiating partners[5/] and hence simplifies the decision making process and reduces the free-rider problem. Bhagwati (1993) countered that larger trading blocks typically have greater market power, impose higher tariffs on each other, and become more inward-looking.[6/] This area still has a lot of potential for future research, and only recently Grossman and Helpman (1994) have addressed some of these questions.

4. Two-Sector Trading Block Model with Comparative Advantage

This two-sector trading block model incorporates the first two lines of criticism, leaving the latter two for future research. My model should remain comparable to Krugman's (1991) model, become more relevant to real world structures, and should remain solvable in a symmetric and comparative-static framework. Hence I will extend the model in two directions:

First, this model retains a market structure of Chamberlinian monopolistic competition and a production of differentiated products, and it includes an element of comparative advantage. This is the combination of Krugman's and

---

5/ 117 parties were negotiating in GATT's Uruguay Round.

6/ Winters (1993), supporting that view, quoted the former EC commissioner for foreign relations, Willy de Clerq, as saying that *"We are not building a single market in order to turn it over to hungry foreigners."*

Ricardo's models, where trade occurs because of product differentiation *and* because of comparative advantage. That comparative advantage exists between differentiated products. More precisely, Ricardo's idea of comparative advantage here is super-imposed on the Dixit-Stiglitz framework of the Krugman model. In other words, this model can be restricted to comparative advantage being zero, but it cannot be restricted to no taste for differentiated products ($\Theta = 1$), since then no trade at all would occur.

We have the option of introducing asymmetric country structures and then develop a probability distribution on what type of countries form trading blocks, which would require a substantial deviation from the Krugman framework and introduce fairly substantial variances. Therefore, we keep a symmetric structure as in Krugman's model, but introduce comparative advantage in the production of individual countries.

The trick in the model design with N countries is to introduce comparative advantage in one industry per country. Symmetry now requires that N industries exist per country so that each of the N countries can have absolute comparative advantage in one industry and a disadvantage in the other (N-1) industries. We label the advanced industry as sector A, and the (N-1) other industries as sector B. That framework designs a two-sector trading block model which keeps Krugman's model as a special case when either no labor is employed in sector B or when the comparative advantage of sector A converges to zero. Our results are hence directly comparable to the results of Krugman's model as a special case.

We introduce comparative advantage in two ways: first, one industry has a production function with lower marginal costs (eg. through better technology) and second, that industry has a higher share of the labor force than all other industries, which creates a so-called home-market effect, as defined by Krugman (1980). Labor remains the only factor of production and is assumed to be immobile both across sectors and across countries. Differences in technology and labor allocation are transmitted into different output x, prices p, wages w, and varieties n. We define again a world consisting of a large number of countries N, which are grouped into a number of symmetric trading blocks C, each consisting of N/C countries. Each country now consists of N industries, which are grouped into two sectors, so that sector A (advanced) contains only the one industry which exhibits comparative advantage in production and which employs a share of δ of the labor force (with $\delta >= 1/N$), and sector B (backward) contains the other (N-1) industries with normal production functions and equal labor shares. That setup is illustrated in figure 2 as an example with N=4 and C=2.

However, our modelling of comparative advantage is limited to the production of one industry in each country. Since labor is immobile, there will be no reallocation and no further specialization after the opening to trade. The open-economy model will only introduce a distortion through tariffs and transport costs. Hence the full benefits from comparative advantage are already realized in autarky, and foreign trade is only beneficial in order to increase the varieties available to the consumer. In a way, that setup is conservative since it underestimates the benefits from free trade, which would be even larger when labor was mobile.

The second extension introduces more carefully modelled tariffs and transport costs. Krugman (1993) already suggested a change from his initial optimal tariff model (1991) and assumed tariffs to be fixed and determined exogenously. However, he still assumed that trading blocks have no internal trade barriers and that transport costs are always zero. In our new trading block model we now assume that tariffs are determined exogenously, which is certainly more realistic that the artificial modelling of optimal tariffs. Therefore, we study two scenarios, one with high tariffs (45%) and one with low tariffs (15%), and show that our results are similar in either setup.

We finally determine the critical level of external tariffs given a certain level of comparative advantage, below which the outcome is a monotonously increasing world welfare (L-shape) and above which the Krugman outcome occurs with a V-shape of world welfare (derived in figure 8). Then we allow more generally for trading blocks to be set up as preferential trading agreements (PTAs) with remaining internal tariffs, and we also introduce transport costs for inter-continental trade. Both extensions include Krugman's model as a special case for these parameters set to zero. With this more sophisticated structure, we then determine by how much the critical tariff level has increased.

Both extensions have been made with the intention to balance two previously extreme and unrealistic assumptions: first, a structure of differentiated products has been balanced by introducing comparative advantage in the production of one industry, and second, a high level of distortionary tariffs has been balanced by allowing the existence of PTAs and inter-block transport costs. The choice of parameters in this model seems to be as important as previously: the parameter Θ indicating the taste for variety is assumed between 0.7 and 0.8, as in Krugman's (1991) original model. The external tariff rate t is assumed to be around 25%, which had been the medium tariff rate (including both tariff and non-tariff barriers) in the simulations of Haveman (1993), and which is higher than the empirical values mentioned in the previous part. We also assume that tariffs ti on intra-block trade are only 5%, which is realistic given the various non-tariff barriers which are remaining even within the European Union. Transport costs g for intra-block trade are assumed to be around 10%, a rather conservative estimate which is lower than the estimates of 20% produced by Frankel, Stein, and Wei (1993). Internal transport costs are assumed to be zero, since they are usually much lower than international transport costs and often offset by positive externalities within blocks, such as R&D spillovers or harmonization effects.

In the following, we first develop the two-sector trading block model including the two above mentioned extensions, where the exposition follows as closely as possible the initial structure of Krugman's model. Only the important steps in the development are presented in the main paper, but details are provided for the closed-economy model in appendix-I and for the open-economy model in appendix-II. Then it is shown that our two-sector model produces the results of Krugman's (1991) model as a special case, and finally the extensions are introduced individually: external tariff scenarios, inter-block transport costs, and internal tariffs.

We define c as the consumption of one individual, and x as the total demand for one product by all consumers. The subscript i indicates the respective product. Moreover, we introduce two other subscripts A and B, where the first subscript denotes the location of the consumer of the product and the second subscript denotes the location of the producer. Hence we obtain the following equations:

$$\begin{aligned} x_{i_A} &= L * c_{i_A} = x_{i_{AA}} + x_{i_{BA}} \\ x_{i_B} &= L * c_{i_B} = x_{i_{AB}} + x_{i_{BB}} \end{aligned} \qquad (13)$$

The market structure is again that of Chamberlinian monopolistic competition and all products are differentiated, while the intensity of the consumer's taste for variety is expressed by the parameter Θ in the utility function (14). The first part represents utility from consuming n_A products produced by one industry in sector A, and the second part the respective utility from consuming n_B products each produced by (N-1) industries in sector B:

$$U = \sum_{i=1}^{n_A} (c_{i_A})^{\theta} + \sum_{k=1}^{N-1} \sum_{i=1}^{n_B} (c_{i_k})^{\theta} \text{ with } 0<\theta<1 \tag{14}$$

As indicated in equations (15), the advanced industry in sector A has a lower variable cost of (ß-s), while each industry in sector B has variable costs of ß. Moreover, labor is assumed to be immobile across sectors, with share δ allocated to sector A and share (1-δ) to sector B. Equations (16) model full employment and solve for the number of produced varieties:

$$\begin{aligned} l_{i_A} &= \alpha + (\beta - s) * x_{i_A} \quad \text{with } \alpha, \beta, s>0 \\ l_{i_k} &= \alpha + \beta * x_{i_k} \qquad \forall k=1\ldots(N-1) \end{aligned} \tag{15}$$

$$\begin{aligned} L_A &= \delta * L = \sum_{i=1}^{n_A} l_{i_A} \rightarrow n_A = \frac{\delta * L}{(c_{i_A})^{\theta}} \\ L_B &= (1-\delta) * L = \sum_{k=1}^{N-1} \sum_{i=1}^{n_B} l_{i_k} \rightarrow n_B = \frac{(1-\delta) * L}{(N-1) * (c_{i_B})^{\theta}} \end{aligned} \tag{16}$$

In a *closed economy*, we can again determine the equilibrium by first deriving the inverse demand function (18) from the maximization problem of a consumer (17), then by deriving the equilibrium prices (20) from the profit maximization of the firms (19), and finally by deriving the equilibrium levels of output (21) from the zero-profit condition. It should be recalled that under Chamberlinian monopolistic competition, each firm has some monopoly power due to product differentiation, but profits are driven to zero by the free entry and exit conditions.

$$\begin{aligned} &Max\ U_A = \sum_{i=1}^{n_A} (c_{i_{AA}})^{\theta} + \sum_{k=1}^{N-1} \sum_{i=1}^{n_B} (c_{i_{Ak}})^{\theta} \\ &s.t.\ \sum_{i=1}^{n_A} (c_{i_{AA}} * p_A) - \sum_{k=1}^{N-1} \sum_{i=1}^{n_B} (c_{i_{Ak}} * p_B) - w_A \geq 0 \end{aligned} \tag{17}$$

$$\begin{aligned} &p_A = \frac{\theta * (c_{i_{AA}})^{\theta-1}}{\lambda} \quad and \quad p_B = \frac{\theta * (c_{i_{Ak}})^{\theta-1}}{\lambda} \\ &hence\ \frac{c_{i_{AA}}}{c_{i_{Ak}}} = \frac{c_{i_{BA}}}{c_{i_{Bk}}} = \left(\frac{p_A}{p_B}\right)^{\left(\frac{1}{\theta-1}\right)} = p^{\left(\frac{1}{\theta-1}\right)} \end{aligned} \tag{18}$$

$$\begin{aligned} &Max\ \pi_{i_A} = p_A * x_{i_A} - w_A * [\alpha + (\beta - s) * x_{i_A}] \\ &with\ \epsilon_i = -\frac{\partial x_{i_A} / x_{i_A}}{\partial p_A / p_A} = \frac{1}{1-\theta} \end{aligned} \tag{19}$$

$$\begin{aligned} &p_A = w_A * \frac{\beta - s}{\theta} \quad and \quad p_B = w_B * \frac{\beta}{\theta} \\ &hence\ \frac{w_A / p_A}{w_B / p_B} = \frac{\beta}{\beta - s} > 1 \end{aligned} \tag{20}$$

$$\begin{aligned} &\pi_{i_A} = p_A * x_{i_A} - w_A * [\alpha + (\beta - s) * x_{i_A}] = 0 \\ &\Leftrightarrow x_{i_A} = \frac{\alpha}{\beta - s} * \frac{\theta}{1-\theta} > x_{i_k} = \frac{\alpha}{\beta} * \frac{\theta}{1-\theta} \end{aligned} \tag{21}$$

Hence real wages in sector A are higher than in sector B, and production in the industry of sector A is higher than in one industry of sector B. Given equilibrium prices and output, the labor market equilibrium (16) determines the equilibrium number of varieties n_A and n_B, as expressed in equations (22). Since labor is the only factor of production and assumed to be immobile, the trade balance between the two sectors must be zero: $n_A * p_A * x_{BA} = n_B * (N-1) * p_B * x_{AB}$ That balance determines relative wages and relative prices as indicated in equations (23):

$$n_A = \frac{(\delta * L) * (1-\theta)}{\alpha} \quad \text{and} \quad n_B = \frac{(1-\delta) * L * (1-\theta)}{\alpha * (N-1)}$$
$$\text{hence} \quad \frac{n_A}{n_B} = \frac{\delta}{1-\delta} * (N-1) \tag{22}$$

$$\frac{w_A}{w_B} = \left(\frac{\beta}{\beta - s}\right)^{\theta} > 1 \quad \text{and} \quad p := \frac{p_A}{p_B} = \left(\frac{\beta - s}{\beta}\right)^{1-\theta} < 1$$
$$\text{hence} \quad \frac{w_A / p_A}{w_B / p_B} = \left(\frac{\beta}{\beta - s}\right) > 1 \tag{23}$$

Once we have determined all these equilibrium values, we can go back to the consumer's budget constraint (17) and calculate the equilibrium consumption of each product, which then determines the consumer's utility (14), as illustrated in detail in appendix-I.

If we now switch from a closed- to an *open-economy model* where N symmetrical countries trade with each other, we expect that output, domestic prices, and varieties do not change, since those variables only depend on parameters as shown in equations (20) to (22). However, we observe two changes: First, consumers consume less of the home products and spend the saved income instead on foreign products in order to increase their utility from more available varieties. World demand and world supply however remain constant, and since labor is immobile, no factor reallocation or specialization can take place. Second, consumers have to pay higher prices for foreign products since transport costs and tariffs must be covered. These differences in prices for home and foreign products imply also different relative demands.

In the following notation, we use the superscripts "h" for the home country, "f" for foreign countries on the same continent (within the same trading block), and "o" for outside countries on another continent (outside the trading block). The first superscript indicates the country demanding goods, whereas the second one indicates the country supplying the goods. We again assume a world with a large number of countries N, which are grouped into C symmetrical trading blocks. We also assume that intra-continental transport costs are zero, but that inter-continental transport costs g of the Samuelson iceberg type occur. Moreover, it is assumed that tariffs are uniform and determined exogenously, that the tariff level for inter-continental trade is t, and that a trading block as a PTA has remaining tariffs for intra-continental trade of ti. All tariff revenue is withheld by the country's authorities and then redistributed in full as a lump-sum transfer back to the consumers.[7/] Equations (24) indicate the prices for the three types of products and equations (25) show the new relative demands σ of foreign or outside products relative to home products:

$$\begin{aligned} p &= p^{hh} = p^{ff} = p^{oo} \\ p_{ti} &= p^{hf} = p^{fh} = p*(1+ti) \\ p_{gt} &= p^{ho} = p^{of} = p*(\frac{1}{1-g}+t) \end{aligned} \tag{24}$$

$$\begin{aligned} \sigma_{A,ti} &= \frac{c_{i_A}^{\,f}}{c_{i_A}^{\,h}} = (\frac{p_A}{p_{A,ti}})^{\frac{1}{1-\theta}} = (1+ti)^{\frac{1}{(\theta-1)}} \\ \sigma_{A,gt} &= (\frac{1}{1-g})*(\frac{p_A}{p_{A,t}})^{\frac{1}{1-\theta}} = (\frac{1}{1-g})*(\frac{1}{1-g}+t)^{\frac{1}{\theta-1}} \end{aligned} \tag{25}$$

Using these prices and relative demands, we must now ensure that consumers respect their budget constraint and that trade between sectors A and B in the aggregate is again balanced, since factors are assumed immobile. The detailed procedure is spelled out in appendix-II. From budget and trade balances we obtain the following key identity (26), which leads to the same relative prices and wages as in the closed economy model (equation 23).

7/ It is assumed that consumers regard the lump-sum transfer as fixed, that means independent of their level of consumption. That simplifying assumption has usually been made in similar models, since otherwise the solutions become quadratic.

$$\frac{c_{i_{AA}}}{c_{i_{BA}}} = \frac{c_{i_{Ak}}}{c_{i_{Bk}}} = \frac{w_A}{w_B} = \left(\frac{p_A}{p_B}\right)^{\left(\frac{\theta}{\theta-1}\right)}$$

$$\frac{c_{i_{AA}}}{c_{i_{Ak}}} = \frac{c_{i_{BA}}}{c_{i_{Bk}}} = \left(\frac{p_A}{p_B}\right)^{\left(\frac{1}{\theta-1}\right)} \qquad (26)$$

We finally turn to the calculation of the different consumption shares, where we first determine one consumption share c_{iAA} from the parameters and then use identities (26) to obtain the remaining consumption shares which we need to calculate the value of the utility function. As it is shown in equation (27), derived in detail in the annexes, the simplified utility function only depends on the parameters of our model.

$$K := \delta + (1-\delta) * p^{\left(\frac{\theta}{1-\theta}\right)} \quad I := \left(\frac{N}{C} - 1\right) * \sigma_{ti} \quad H := \left(N - \frac{N}{C}\right) * \sigma_{gt}$$

$$U = \left[\delta + (1-\delta) * \left(\frac{\beta - s}{\beta}\right)^{\theta * \theta}\right] * \left(\frac{1-\theta}{\alpha}\right) * L * K * [1 + I + H] \; * \; (c_{i_{AA}})^{\theta} \qquad (27)$$

$$U = U(\alpha, \beta, s, \delta, \theta, t, ti, g, L, N, C)$$

numeraires	$\alpha := 1$	$\beta := 1$	$L := 1$	$w_A := 1$	$N := 60$
variables	$s \in [0,1]$	$\delta \in [0,1]$	$\theta \in [0.70, 0.80]$	$C \in [1,60]$	
	$t \in [0.15, 0.45]$	$ti \in [0, 0.05]$	$g \in [0, 0.1]$		

The results of our trading block model are now illustrated in four steps: first, we solve it for the special case of Krugman's one-sector model, second we study two tariff scenarios in our two-sector framework, then we introduce transport costs, and finally we add internal tariffs. That sequence is useful in order to understand what changes compared to Krugman's setup are driving the results and how sensitive results are to changes in parameters. Starting with Krugman's one-sector model as a special case, we consider only one sector by setting $\delta=0$ and we assume no scale economies by setting $s=0$. Moreover, as in Krugman's (1991) original model, we abstract from transport costs ($g=0$) and internal tariffs ($ti=0$). That only leaves two variables in our utility function, which are tariffs t and the taste for variety Θ. The results are illustrated in figure 3 for tariffs of 25% or 30% and for $\Theta \epsilon [0.70, 0.80]$.

The results are very similar to Krugman's (1991 and 1993) results, with a welfare minimum in the presence of three trading blocks and a V-shaped form of the welfare function. Maximum gains from free trade range from 3% to 4% of total welfare, which is a typical outcome for a trade model, but much lower than we would expect in reality. Figure 3 also tells us about the reasonable range of parameters: the upper graph with a modest taste for variety (higher Θ of 0.80) shows a sharp V-shape and suggests that welfare under isolation is higher than under free-trade, which is counter-intuitive, while the lower graph with a strong taste for variety (lower Θ of 0.70) shows a very flat V-shape for the welfare function. In reality, the shape should be in between these two extremes, which suggests a value for the taste of variety around $\Theta=0.75$ [medium value used by Krugman (1991)] and a value of taxes around $t=0.25$.

In the following three applications, we keep Krugman's one-sector model as one scenario, and compare it with two scenarios of our two-sector model: the *Krugman scenario* assumes that all labor is employed in sector A with scale economies of 20% (δ=1.00; s=0.20) ; the *partial specialization scenario* assumes that only half the labor force is employed in sector A with scale economies of 40% and the other half is employed in sector B without any scale economies (δ=0.50; s=0.40) ; and the *full specialization scenario* assumes that only one quarter of the labor force is employed in sector A with scale economies of 80% (δ=0.25; s=0.80). All three scenarios hence produce average scale economies of 20% per worker, which is helpful for the comparison of the outcomes. It should be recalled that in our model the term scale economies refers to reduced variable costs, while it normally refers to effects of reduced fixed or sunk costs. The assumption that variable costs can be reduced by up to 80% seems challenging, but not unrealistic, if we consider wage differentials for instance between the United States and Mexico or between Germany and Hungary which in some sectors exceed the ratio of 10:1.

The *first application A* reveals how sensitive our results are to the level of tariffs: Figure 4 presents a high-tariff scenario with t=0.45, which is similar to the medium case of Krugman's (1991) original model under the assumption of optimal tariffs. The upper graph shows the typical Krugman case, with a minimum at three trading blocks and a V-shaped welfare function.[8/] The partial specialization scenario reveals a much flatter V-shape, now with a minimum at five blocks, while the full specialization case reveals a monotonously rising welfare from progressing integration. Moreover, the gains from free trade under full specialization are three times higher than in the Krugman scenario[9/]. That illustration clarifies the most important result, which is consistent with the intuition developed in part 2: Our two-sector trading block model includes Krugman's model as a special case and reproduces his results, and it shows that under specialization even in the presence of high external tariffs, progressing integration (from 60 blocks towards one block) monotonously increases world welfare (L-shaped function).

Figure 5 strengthens that key result by revealing that under lower external tariffs, now set at t=0.15, a function of monotonously increasing world welfare evolves even under lower specialization. Moreover, we see that under lower external tariffs Krugman's scenario changes to an essentially flat curve, with nearly no difference in welfare between situations of three trading blocks and isolation. However, the welfare minimum remains, in that case at five blocks.

8/ In the original Krugman model, however, delta was zero, and hence the level of welfare under isolation (C=N=60) would only reach 0.97. (here with delta=1 we have an artifact).

9/ Each scenario has been normalized to include the datapoint (1,1). Without normalization, the graph of the full specialization scenario would have reached the welfare axis at point (1,1.2).

Resuming, our first application A shows that in a two-sector trading block model, world welfare does increase monotonously from sequential regional integration if significant comparative advantage exists. The extent of comparative advantage required for this result becomes lower when we reduce the level of the external tariff. Moreover, potential gains from free trade are substantially larger in the presence of comparative advantage.

So far we assumed that trade among all countries is without cost. In reality, there are significant transportation costs, although their level has declined over the last decades.[10/] Moreover, transportation costs vary among different trading partners, while those costs among neighboring countries are close to zero, they are substantial if shipping between continents is required. Frankel, Stein, and Wei (1993, page 44) estimated that the differential between inter- and intra-continental transport costs is about 20%. The absence of any transport costs in our previous application biased the outcome in two ways: first, trade between countries of different blocks was higher than in the presence of transport costs, and hence the extent of trade diversion was exaggerated; and second, the potential benefits from free trade were understated.

10/ Transportation costs should probably be understood as transaction costs, including physical transportation, communication costs, and administrative costs which reveal that countries tend to have more similarities with neighbors and their institutions. That notion was proposed by Stein and Frankel (1993, page 9).

Figure 6 illustrates again our three scenarios for the *second application B*, where external tariffs are at t=0.25 and inter-continental transport costs are g=0.20. In this graph, however, the three scenarios are no longer normalized to one, so that the welfare gains from increased specialization are immediately visible. In the Krugman scenario, the welfare function is again basically flat at the right end, but in this case the minimum shifted to 13 blocks and the shape of the graph has become very similar to the graph of the scenario with partial specialization. Moreover, the full specialization scenario reveals two further insights: Potential benefits from free trade are 30% higher than in the Krugman scenario, and a significant part of these benefits have already been achieved in a system of three trading blocks, since the increase in the welfare function in the full specialization scenario has become more gradual.

Basically the same results are obtained in our *third application C*, which is illustrated in figure 7: In this case we have reduced transport costs to g=0.10 and introduced an internal tariff of ti=0.05, allowing for possible preferential trading areas. In reality, most trading blocks are not free trade areas, but rather preferential trading areas with some remaining internal trade barriers, such as administrative procedures, different standards, etc. Therefore this application should be closest to real world structures: it models comparative advantage, external tariffs are determined exogenously at a medium level of 25%, remaining internal tariff barriers are 5%, and inter-continental transport costs are 10%.

Table 4 summarizes our findings and provides a comparison of potential gains from free trade under the three scenarios. We distinguish three areas of the welfare function: the right area from 60 to 12 blocks, the center area from 12 to 3 blocks, and the left area from 3 to 1 blocks. In all scenarios, the welfare function is basically flat in the right area. While the welfare function in the Krugman scenario also remains flat in the center area, it starts increasing faster in that area under more specialization. In application C for example, the Krugman scenario reveals that only 4% of the total potential welfare gains have been achieved under three trading blocks, while that ratio reaches 27% in the case of partial specialization, and 35% in the case of full specialization. In that latter case, total potential welfare gains from free trade are more than twice the size compared to the Krugman scenario.

Finally, we need to decide which parameters are essential in our model, and which are the critical values where our L-shaped word welfare function switches to a Krugman U-shaped world welfare function. Figure 8 illustrates that parameter field: First assume that no internal tariffs ti exist and that no transaction cost g exist (lower line). Then given any level of comparative advantage s (horizontal axis), there does exist one critical external tariff t (vertical axis), below which the welfare function is L-shaped (area B) and above which it is V-shaped (area A). As we can see in figure 8, when Krugman assumed zero comparative advantage, any tariff t above 6.4% produces a V-shaped welfare function.

Table 4: Comparison of Gains from Free-trade under Specialization

Application A: no transport costs, no internal tariff, tariff rate t=0.25, Θ=0.75 (corresponding to intermediate case of figures 4 and 5):

	Total	Right	Center	Left	Ratio
concentr. δ=0.25; scale s=0.80	11.9	+0.74	+3.10	+8.05	32%
concentr. δ=0.40; scale s=0.50	6.47	-0.17	+0.97	+5.66	12%
concentr. δ=1.00; scale s=0.20	1.13	-1.16	-1.20	+3.49	negative

Application B: transport costs g=0.20, no internal tariff, tariff rate t=0.25, Θ=0.75 (corresponding to figure 6):

	Total	Right	Center	Left	Ratio
concentr. δ=0.25; scale s=0.80	22.0	+1.8	+6.71	+13.	39%
concentr. δ=0.40; scale s=0.50	17.4	+0.8	+4.77	+11.	32%
concentr. δ=1.00; scale s=0.20	12.8	-0.38	+2.83	+10.	19%

Application C: transport costs g=0.10, int.tariff ti=0.05, tariff rate t=0.25, Θ=0.75 (corresponding to figure 7):

	Total	Right	Center	Left	Ratio
concentr. δ=0.25; scale s=0.80	14.2	+1.0	+3.97	+9.2	35%
concentr. δ=0.40; scale s=0.50	9.99	+0.3	+2.31	+7.3	27%
concentr. δ=1.00; scale s=0.20	5.80	-0.38	+0.63	+5.5	4%

<u>**Notes:**</u> Total: percentage of free-trade-welfare achieved by transition from isolation to free trade
Right: percentage of free-trade-welfare achieved by integrating from 60 to 12 trading blocks
Center: percentage of free-trade-welfare achieved by integrating from 12 to 3 trading blocks
Left: percentage of free-trade-welfare achieved by integrating from 3 to 1 trading blocks
Ratio: ratio of "Right" plus "Center" welfare gains over "Total" welfare gains.

In the presence of medium comparative advantage (s=0.40), the external tariff t needs to be at least 19.9% for a V-shaped world welfare function to result. In other words, given at least medium comparative advantage (s>0.40) *or* below average external tariffs (t<0.20), world welfare becomes monotonously increasing (L-shaped). Now assume more realistically that internal tariffs ti are 5% and transaction costs g are 10% (lower curve). The curve of critical tariffs then shifts upwards to the left, and the space B becomes much larger: even in the presence of low comparative advantage (s=0.20) and above average tariff levels (up to 23%), the resulting welfare function is monotonously increasing (L-shaped). Figure 9 illustrates the same parameter fields with the resulting number of trading blocks where welfare is minimized. Inside field B (in figure 8), world welfare is monotonously increasing, and hence minimum world welfare occurs in isolation at C=N=60 trading blocks (shown in figure 9). Inside field A (in figure 8), world welfare has an internal minimum, which occurs at C=3 trading blocks when we are in the far upper-left corner, and which approaches C=60 trading blocks when we get closer to the separation line (illustrated in figure 9).

We can summarize three important findings from the analysis of our trading block model: First, in a world where comparative advantage exists, sequential regional integration from isolation towards free trade can monotonously increase the level of world welfare, and in our symmetric model it also increases the level of each individual's welfare. Second, regional integration becomes more beneficial in the presence of higher comparative advantage, and potential gains from free-trade can be double of those available without any comparative advantage. Third, our model suggests that under the current system of three main trading blocks and under present average tariff levels, about one third of potential gains from free trade have already been realized.

5. A BRIEF CRITIQUE, CONCLUSIONS, AND OUTLOOK

We developed a two-sector trading block model which extended Krugman's symmetric one-sector model by introducing comparative advantage, but some shortcomings are remaining: especially the assumptions that labor is the only factor of production and that it is immobile across sectors and countries are unsatisfactory. Consequently, output and domestic prices do not change in an open-economy model, and no further specialization is possible. Comparative advantage is only beneficial in the specialization of production in autarky, while trade is beneficial by increasing varieties. Potential benefits from free-trade would be even larger if factors can be reallocated and production further specialized. However, that shortcoming in a way strengthens our results, since benefits from free-trade would be even larger in a model with mobile factors of production. The crucial difference in our model of comparative advantage compared to Krugman's (1991) model is that we eliminated the previous bias of exaggerated trade diversion which was implied by Krugman's "Armington-assumption".

Moreover, the two lines of criticism which have been brought forward against Krugman's model also apply in this case: First, our model assumes symmetric structures of countries, an assumption hard to relax if we still want to be able to solve the model in a non-stochastic way. However, it is possible to proceed from the symmetric equilibrium and to study the effects when the relative size of trading blocks is changed and one block sequentially expands by integrating members of other blocks. That approach will likely involve a large number of simulations and less certainty in its results because of the large variance which is introduced. Second, our model has been elaborated in a comparative-static framework, and it could be extended into a dynamic setting by incorporating some features from the political economy of integration. That extension would further enhance our understanding on how regional arrangements change the environment for sequential multilateral liberalization.

The results of our simulations widely coincide with the intuition we gained from looking at trade data. We concluded that both in theory and post-war reality, regional integration has had small, but positive effects on world welfare. The ongoing multilateral integration of the world economy has apparently not been hindered by regional trade policies which evolved especially in Europe, since the volumes of both intra- and extra-regional trade increased. Our simulations confirm that regionalism and multilateralism can be compatible and can enhance world welfare. Our results illustrate that in the presence of comparative advantage and around average tariff levels, sequential regional integration monotonously improves world welfare.

Moreover, our trading block model shows that potential benefits from integration are much larger if comparative advantage is significant, suggesting that regional agreements among dissimilar countries, ceteris paribus, produce larger welfare gains. Finally, assuming that the world reveals a relatively large degree of comparative advantage across industries and countries, and present average tariffs levels are around 20%, our simulations show that under a system of three symmetrical trading blocks, already one third of the potential benefits from free trade have been realized.

Although the results from our trading block model are in many ways rather suggestive than conclusive, they have some important policy implications. One analogy may be illustrative: The original one-sector trading block model by Krugman only allows for intra-industry trade (eg. trading green apples for red apples). In our framework, we model two sectors and give each country absolute comparative advantage in one industry, hence allowing for inter-industry trade (eg. trading apples for cars). Each country has net exports of its products in the most competitive industry (sector A) and has net imports of all other products. In reality, up to 80% of trade among industrialized countries represents intra-industry trade, while trade with or between developing countries reveals shares of inter-industry trade of usually more than 50%.

This model does not advocate regionalism at any price, for instance regional arrangements under colonial ties may have been welfare reducing, since gains from higher comparative advantage may have been more than offset by higher transport costs and regulations. Moreover, it does not advocate managed regional trade, as we observed it during the 1960s and 1970s in many parts of Africa and Latin America, with forced specialization in production and managed investment flows. That environment would completely change the structural form of our model and it would also tremendously increase transaction costs.

On the other hand, the results from our model might be good news for advocates of NAFTA and of the Central European integration into the European Union. Both regions include countries with very different sizes and incomes per capita, suggesting that gains from larger comparative advantage may be substantial. Moreover, the partner countries in these regions are natural partners, and the agreements aim to be implemented on the basis of market economics, so that transaction costs should not increase significantly. Both Mexico and Central European economies have a high share of inter-industry trade, and, if lessons from the Southern European enlargement are applicable (eg. Winters and Venables, 1991), the largest gains from integration accumulate in those industries with high inter-industry trade. But these final remarks are more speculative, since our assumptions of symmetry are not well applicable in the real world.

6. REFERENCES

Anderson, Kym and Richard Blackhurst. (1993). *"Regional Integration and the Global Trading System"*. St.Martins Press. New York.

Anderson, Kym and Hege Norheim. (1993). "Is World Trade Becoming More Regionalized". *Review of International Economics*. 1(2): 91-109.

Baldwin, Richard. (1989). "The Growth Effects of 1992". *Economic Policy*. 9: 247-281.

Baldwin, Richard. (1992). "An Eastern Enlargement of EFTA". mimeo. Graduate Institute of International Studies. Geneva.

Baldwin, Richard. (1993) "A Domino Theory of Regionalism". NBER Working Paper No. 4465. Cambridge, Massachusetts.

Bhagwati, Jagdish (1990). "Multilateralism at Risk: The GATT is dead, long live GATT". *The World Economy*. 13: 149-169.

Bhagwati, Jagdish (1992). *"Regionalism and Multilateralism"*. CEPR and The World Bank.

Bhagwati, Jagdish (1993). *"Regionalism and Multilateralism: an overview"*. in: Jaime De Melo and Arvind Panagariya (eds): "New Dimensions in Regional Integration". CEPR and University of Cambridge: Cambridge (UK).

Blackhurst, Richard, and David Henderson. (1993). *"Regional Integration Agreements, World Integration, and the GATT"*. in: Kym Anderson and Richard Blackhurst (eds): "Regional Integration and the Global Trading System". St.Martins Press. New York.

Bond, Eric W. and Constantinos Syropoulos. (1993). "Optimality and Stability of Regional Trading Blocks". mimeo. Pennsylvania State University.

Centre for Economic Policy Research (CEPR). (1992). "*Is bigger better? The Economics of EC Enlargement*". CEPR: London.

De la Torre, Augusto, and Margaret R. Kelly. (1992). "*Regional Trade Arrangements*". Occasional Paper No. 92. International Monetary Fund. Washington DC.

De Melo, Jaime and Arvind Panagariya. (1993). "*New Dimensions in Regional Integration*". CEPR and University of Cambridge: Cambridge (UK).

Deardorff, Alan V. and Robert M. Stern. (1992). "Multilateral Trade Negotiations and Preferential Trading Arrangements". Discussion Paper No. 307. University of Michigan.

Dixit, L. and J. Stiglitz. (1977). "Monopolistic Competition and Optimum Product Diversity". *American Economic Review.* 67: 297-308.

Flemming, John and J.M.C. Rollo. (1992). "*Trade, Payments, and Adjustment in Central and Eastern Europe*". Royal Institute of International Affairs: London.

Frankel, Jeffrey, Ernesto Stein and Shang-Jin Wei. (1993). "Trading Blocks: The Natural, the Unnatural, and the Super-Natural". mimeo. International Monetary Fund. Washington DC.

Frankel, Jeffrey and Shang-Jin Wei. (1992). "Yen Bloc or Dollar Bloc: Exchange Rate Policies of the East Asian Economies". mimeo. NBER.

Fratzscher, Oliver. (1994). "European Integration: Lessons from the South and Prospects for the East". in Schipke and Taylor (eds.): "*The Economics of Transformation: Theory and Practice in the New Market Economies*". Springer: New York. 191-232.

Grossman, Gene and Elhanan Helpman. (1993). "The Politics of Free Trade Agreements". NBER Working Paper No. 4597. Cambridge, Massachusetts.

Grossman, Gene and Elhanan Helpman. (1994). "Protection for Sale". *American Economic Review*. forthcoming.

Haaland, Jan I. (1993). "Welfare Effects of 1992: a General Equilibrium Assessment for EC and EFTA Countries. mimeo. Norwegian School of Economics and Business Administration.

Hamilton, Carl B. and Alan L. Winters. (1992). "Trade with Eastern Europe". *Economic Policy*. 12: 77-116.

Haveman, Jon D. (1993). "Some Welfare Effects of Sequential Customs Union Formation". mimeo. Purdue University.

Helpman, Elhanan and Paul R. Krugman. (1985). *"Market Structure and Foreign Trade"*. MIT Press: Cambridge, Massachusetts.

Irwin, Douglas A. (1992). "Multilateral and Bilateral Trade Policies in the World Trading System: An Historical Perspective". Conference on Regional Integration. The World Bank: Washington DC.

Kemp, Murray C. and Henry Y. Wan. (1976). "An Elementary Proposition Concerning the Formation of Customs Unions". *Journal of International Economics*. 6: 95-97.

Krugman, Paul R. (1979). "Increasing Returns, Monopolistic Competition and International Trade". *Journal of International Economics*. 9: 469-479.

Krugman, Paul R. (1980). "Scale Economies, Product Differentiation, and the Pattern of Trade". *American Economic Review*. 70: 950-959.

Krugman, Paul R. (1991a). "Is Bilateralism bad?". in E. Helpman and A. Razin (eds.) *"International Trade and Trade Policy"*. MIT Press: Cambridge, Massachusetts.

Krugman, Paul R. (1991b). "The Move toward Free Trade Zones". *Economic Review* (Kansas). November 1991: 5-25.

Krugman, Paul R. (1993). *"Regionalism versus Multilateralism: analytical notes"*. in: Jaime De Melo and Arvind Panagariya (eds): "New Dimensions in regional integration". CEPR and University of Cambridge: Cambridge (UK).

Lawrence, Robert Z. (1991). "Emerging Regional Arrangements: Building Blocks or Stumbling Blocks?". in: *"Finance and the International Economy"*. Amex Bank Review. Oxford University Press: Oxford.

Lawrence, Robert Z. (1994). "Regionalism, Multilateralism, and Deeper Integration". mimeo. Harvard University: Cambridge, Massachusetts.

Leamer, Edward E. (1992). "Testing Trade Theory". NBER Working Paper No. 3958. Cambridge, Massachusetts.

Lipsey, R. (1957). "The Theory of Customs Unions: Trade Diversion and Welfare". *Economica*. 24: 40-46.

Meade, J. (1955). *"The Theory of Customs Unions"*. North Holland: Amsterdam.

Norman, Victor D. and Anthony J. Venables. (1993). "International Trade, Factor Mobility, and Trade Costs". CEPR Discussion Paper No. 766.

OECD Development Centre. (1993). "Trade Liberalization: what's at stake ?". by Ian Goldin and D. van der Mensbrugghe. OECD Policy Brief No. 5.

Perroni, Carlo and John Whalley. (1994). "The new Regionalism: Trade Liberalization or Insurance?". NBER Working Paper No. 4626. January 1994. Cambridge, Massachusetts.

Ricardo, David. (1971). (first published in 1817). *"The Principles of Political Economy and Taxation"*. Penguin: Baltimore.

Rollo, Jim and Alasdair Smith. (1993). "EC Trade with Eastern Europe". *Economic Policy*. April 1993. 13: 139-181.

Srinivasan, T.N. (1993). "Comments to Paul Krugman". in: Jaime De Melo and Arvind Panagariya (eds): "New Dimensions in Regional Integration". CEPR and University of Cambridge: Cambridge (UK).

Srinivasan, T.N., John Whalley, and Ian Wooton. (1993). *"Measuring the Effects of Regionalism on Trade and Welfare"*. in: Kym Anderson and Richard Blackhurst (eds): "Regional Integration and the Global Trading System". St.Martins Press. New York.

Stein, Ernesto and Jeffrey Frankel. (1993). "Transport Costs and the Welfare Implications of Free Trade Agreements". mimeo. University of California, Berkeley.

Summers, Lawrence H. (1991). *"Regionalism and the World Trading System"*. in Summers (ed): "Policy Implications of Trade and Currency Zones". Federal Reserye Bank of Kansas City.

Viner, Jacob. (1950). *"The Customs Union Issue"*. Carnegie Endowment for International Peace: New York.

Winters, L. Alan and Anthony Venables. (1991). *"European Integration: Trade and Industry"*. Cambridge University Press: Cambridge.

Winters, L. Alan. (1993). *"The European Community: a Case of Successful Integration?"*. in: Jaime De Melo and Arvind Panagariya (eds): "New Dimensions in Regional Integration". CEPR and University of Cambridge: Cambridge (UK).

Wonnacott, Paul and Mark Lutz. (1989). "Is there a Case for Free Trade Areas?" in Jeffrey Schott (ed.) *"Free Trade Areas and U.S. Trade Policy"*. Institute for International Economics: Washington DC.

Wooton, Ian. (1986). "Preferential Trading Arrangements: an investigation". *Journal of International Economics*. 21: 81-97.

7. APPENDIX-I: TWO-SECTOR CLOSED ECONOMY MODEL

<A> Consumer Maximizes Utility Subject to Budget Constraint:

$$Max\ U_A = \sum_{i=1}^{n_A} (c_{i_{AA}})^\theta + \sum_{k=1}^{N-1} \sum_{i=1}^{n_B} (c_{i_{Ak}})^\theta$$

$$s.t.\ BC_A = \sum_{i=1}^{n_A} (c_{i_{AA}} * p_A) + \sum_{k=1}^{N-1} \sum_{i=1}^{n_B} (c_{i_{Ak}} * p_B)\ - w_A \geq 0 \qquad \text{(A-1)}$$

$$in\ Lagrange\ form:\ \ MAX\ L_A = U_A - \lambda * BC_A$$

Here we only demonstrate the procedure for consumer A (it is analogous for consumer B). From partial derivatives we obtain:

$$p_A = \frac{\theta * (c_{i_{AA}})^{\theta-1}}{\lambda} \quad and \quad p_B = \frac{\theta * (c_{i_{Ak}})^{\theta-1}}{\lambda}$$

$$hence\ \ \frac{c_{i_{AA}}}{c_{i_{Ak}}} = \frac{c_{i_{BA}}}{c_{i_{Bk}}} = \left(\frac{p_A}{p_B}\right)^{\left(\frac{1}{\theta-1}\right)} = p^{\left(\frac{1}{\theta-1}\right)} \qquad \text{(A-2)}$$

<B> Producer Maximizes Profits Given Its Cost:

First, we need to calculate the elasticity, which is constant because of the CES utility function:

$$x_{i_A} = \delta * L * c_{i_{AA}} + (1-\delta) * L * c_{i_{BA}}$$

$$= \delta * L * \left(\frac{\lambda * p_A}{\theta}\right)^{\left(\frac{1}{\theta-1}\right)} + (1-\delta) * L * \left(\frac{\mu * p_A}{\theta}\right)^{\left(\frac{1}{\theta-1}\right)} \qquad \text{(A-3)}$$

$$hence\ \ \epsilon_i = -\frac{\partial x_{i_A} / x_{i_A}}{\partial p_A / p_A} = \frac{\partial x_{i_A} / \partial p_A}{x_{i_A} / p_A} = \frac{1}{1-\theta} \quad (CES)$$

Then we maximize the producer's profits, knowing the cost schedule:

$$\begin{aligned} &Max\ \pi_{i_A} = p_A * x_{i_A} - w_A * [\alpha + (\beta - s) * x_{i_A}] \\ &\frac{\delta \pi_{i_A}}{\delta p_A} = x_{i_A} + p_A * \frac{\delta x_{i_A}}{\delta p_A} - w_A * (\beta - s) * \frac{\delta x_{i_A}}{\delta p_A} \\ &\quad = x_{i_A} * [1 + (1 - (\beta - s) * \frac{w_A}{p_A}) * \frac{1}{\theta - 1}] = 0 \end{aligned} \tag{A-4}$$

Finally, we can solve that equation for the price. We find a mark-up pricing behavior since $\theta < 1$, which implies a price larger than marginal cost. Moreover, relative wages are equal to relative marginal productivity.

$$\begin{aligned} &p_A = w_A * \frac{\beta - s}{\theta} \quad and \quad p_B = w_B * \frac{\beta}{\theta} \\ &hence \quad \frac{w_A / p_A}{w_B / p_B} = \frac{\beta}{\beta - s} > 1 \end{aligned} \tag{A-5}$$

<C> Monopolistic Competition with Free Entry Drive Equilibrium Profits to Zero:

$$\begin{aligned} &\pi_{i_A} = p_A * x_{i_A} - w_A * [\alpha + (\beta - s) * x_{i_A}] = 0 \\ &\leftrightarrow x_{i_A} = \frac{\alpha}{p_A / w_A - (\beta - s)} = \frac{\alpha * \theta}{(\beta - s) * (1 - \theta)} \\ &\leftrightarrow x_{i_A} = \frac{\alpha}{\beta - s} * \frac{\theta}{1 - \theta} > x_{i_k} = \frac{\alpha}{\beta} * \frac{\theta}{1 - \theta} \end{aligned} \tag{A-6}$$

The zero profit condition hence determines equilibrium output, which combined with labor market equilibrium determines the number of produced varieties:

$$\begin{aligned} &L_A = \delta * L = \sum_{i=1}^{n_A} l_A = n_A * [\alpha + (\beta - s) * x_{i_A}] = n_A * \alpha * (1 + \frac{\theta}{1 - \theta}) \\ &hence\ n_A = \frac{(\delta * L) * (1 - \theta)}{\alpha} \quad and \quad n_B = \frac{(1 - \delta) * L * (1 - \theta)}{\alpha * (N - 1)} \\ &therefore \quad \frac{n_A}{n_B * (N - 1)} = \frac{\delta}{1 - \delta} \end{aligned} \tag{A-7}$$

<D> Budget Balance and Trade Balance Determine Relative Prices and Consumption Shares:

Each individual spends the entire wages on products from both sectors. With help of equation (A-2), we can then determine the ratio of the two consumption shares:

$$n_A * p_A * c_{i_{AA}} + n_B * (N-1) * p_B * c_{i_{Ak}} = w_A \;;\; n_A * p_A * c_{i_{BA}} + n_B * (N-1) * p_B * c_{i_{Bk}} = w_B$$

$$c_{i_{AA}} = \frac{w_A}{n_A * p_A + n_B * (N-1) * p^{(\frac{1}{1-\theta})}} \quad and \quad c_{i_{BA}} = \frac{w_B}{n_A * p_A + n_B * (N-1) * p^{(\frac{1}{1-\theta})}} \qquad \text{(A-8)}$$

$$n_A * p_A * x_{i_{BA}} = n_B * (N-1) * p_B * x_{i_{Ak}} \quad with \;\; x_{i_{BA}} = (1-\delta) * L * c_{i_{BA}}$$

$$\leftrightarrow \frac{c_{i_{Ak}}}{c_{i_{BA}}} = \frac{n_A}{n_B * (N-1)} * (\frac{1-\delta}{\delta}) * \frac{p_A}{p_B} = p \quad with \;\; \frac{c_{i_{AA}}}{c_{i_{Ak}}} = p^{(\frac{1}{\theta-1})} \qquad \text{(A-9)}$$

$$\leftrightarrow \frac{c_{i_{AA}}}{c_{i_{BA}}} = p^{(\frac{\theta}{\theta-1})} \leftrightarrow p = (\frac{c_{i_{AA}}}{c_{i_{BA}}})^{(\frac{\theta-1}{\theta})}$$

Since labor and capital are immobile across sectors, trade must be balanced, which implies that the value of goods B purchased by A must be equal to the value of goods A purchased by B.

From equations (A-8) and (A-9), we can now determine relative prices:

$$p = \frac{p_A}{p_B} = (\frac{c_{i_{AA}}}{c_{i_{BA}}})^{(\frac{\theta-1}{\theta})} = (\frac{w_A}{w_B})^{(\frac{\theta-1}{\theta})} \;;\; \frac{p_A}{p_B} = (\frac{w_A}{w_B}) * (\frac{\beta - s}{\beta})$$

$$hence \;\; \frac{w_A}{w_B} = (\frac{\beta}{\beta - s})^{\theta} > 1 \;;\; \frac{p_A}{p_B} = (\frac{\beta - s}{\beta})^{1-\theta} < 1 \qquad \text{(A-10)}$$

$$hence \;\; \frac{w_A / p_A}{w_B / p_B} = (\frac{\beta}{\beta - s}) > 1$$

This indicates that lower cost and higher productivity in sector A imply that products A are priced lower than products B, and wages are higher in sector A.

<E> Consumption Shares Determine Value of the Utility Function and Country's Welfare:

Starting from the budget constraint of an individual in sector A, we replace wages, prices, and varieties with the results from the previous sections and determine one consumption share c_{iAA}:

$$c_{i_{AA}} = \frac{w_A / p_A}{n_A + n_B * (N-1) * p^{-1} * p^{1/(1-\theta)}}$$

$$\Rightarrow \quad c_{i_{AA}} = \frac{\theta}{(\beta - s)} * 1 / [\delta * L * \frac{(1-\theta)}{\alpha} + (1-\delta) * L * \frac{(1-\theta)}{\alpha} * p^{(\frac{\theta}{1-\theta})}] \qquad \text{(A-11)}$$

$$\textit{defining} \quad K := \delta + (1-\delta) * p^{(\frac{\theta}{1-\theta})} \quad \textit{and} \quad K \in [0,1]$$

$$\Leftrightarrow \quad c_{i_{AA}} = (\frac{\alpha}{\beta - s}) * (\frac{\theta}{1-\theta}) * \frac{1}{L} * \frac{1}{K} \quad = \quad c_{i_{AA}}(\alpha, \beta, s, \delta, \theta, L)$$

Let us now recall the relationship between the consumption shares: consumer A's relative consumption of products A and B was determined in part <B> from consumers maximization, and the relative consumption of products A by consumers A and B was determined in part <D> from the budget constraints:

$$\frac{c_{i_{AA}}}{c_{i_{Ak}}} = \frac{c_{i_{BA}}}{c_{i_{Bk}}} = p^{(\frac{1}{\theta-1})} = (\frac{\beta}{\beta - s}) > 1$$

$$\frac{c_{i_{AA}}}{c_{i_{BA}}} = \frac{c_{i_{Ak}}}{c_{i_{Bk}}} = p^{(\frac{\theta}{\theta-1})} = \frac{w_A}{w_B} = (\frac{\beta}{\beta - s})^{\theta} > 1 \qquad \text{(A-12)}$$

We can simplify the utility function as a function of one consumption share c_{iAA}:

$$U_A = \sum_{i=1}^{n_A} (c_{i_{AA}})^{\theta} + \sum_{k=1}^{N-1} \sum_{i=1}^{n_B} (c_{i_{Ak}})^{\theta} = n_A * (c_{i_{AA}})^{\theta} + (N-1) * n_B * (c_{i_{Ak}})^{\theta}$$

$$\Rightarrow \quad U_A = [\, n_A + (N-1) * n_B * (\frac{\beta - s}{\beta})^{\theta} \,] * (c_{i_{AA}})^{\theta} \qquad \text{(A-13)}$$

$$U = \delta * U_A + (1-\delta) * U_B = U_A * [\delta + (1-\delta) * (\frac{w_B}{w_A})^{\theta}] = U(\alpha, \beta, s, \delta, \theta, L)$$

8. APPENDIX-II: TWO-SECTOR OPEN ECONOMY MODEL

<A> Tariffs and Transportation Costs Determine Relative Demand for Non-domestic Products:

Figure 2 illustrates the open-economy model of trading blocks, where N countries are grouped into C blocks: Country 1 is the home country, countries 2 to (N/C) are foreign countries within the same trading block, and countries (N/C+1) to N are outside countries grouped into (C-1) outside trading blocks. This structure implies differences to the closed-economy model because of tariffs and transport costs, however, the basic elements of our model in appendix I (parts <A> through <C>) are remaining. First, we determine the prices p and relative demands σ, and distinguish countries within the same trading block facing only low intra-block tariffs ti, and countries outside facing both transport costs g and tariffs t (identified by subscript gt). We assume that tariffs are set exogenously, and that tariff revenue is redistributed as a lump-sum transfer to consumers. We also define three help variables I,H, and K for more ease of exposition:

$$p_{ti} = p*(1+ti) \quad and \quad p_{gt} = p*(\frac{1}{1-g}+t)$$

$$\sigma_{A,ti} = \frac{c_{i_A}^{\ f}}{c_{i_A}^{\ h}} = (\frac{p_A}{p_{A,ti}})^{\frac{1}{1-\theta}} = (1+ti)^{\frac{1}{(\theta-1)}} \qquad \text{(A-14)}$$

$$\sigma_{A,gt} = (\frac{1}{1-g})*(\frac{p_A}{p_{A,t}})^{\frac{1}{1-\theta}} = (\frac{1}{1-g})*(\frac{1}{1-g}+t)^{\frac{1}{\theta-1}}$$

$$I := (\frac{N}{C}-1)*\sigma_{ti} \quad H := (N-\frac{N}{C})*\sigma_{gt} \quad K := \delta+(1-\delta)*p^{(\frac{\theta}{1-\theta})}$$

<B> Budget Balance and Trade Balance Determine Relative Prices and Consumption Shares:

First, we determine the value of the per-capita lump-sum transfer from tariff revenues, which we can simplify using the properties from equations (A-12), so that it can be expressed as a function of only one consumption share:

$$T = (\delta*L)*(ti*I+t*H)*[n_A*p_A*c_{i_{AA}}+n_B*(N-1)*p_B*c_{i_{Ak}}] + (1-\delta)*L*(ti*I+t*H)*[n_A*p_A*c_{i_{BA}}+n_B*(N-1)*p_B*c_{i_{Bk}}] \quad \text{(A-15)}$$

$$T/L = [\delta+(1-\delta)*p^{(\frac{\theta}{1-\theta})}]*[ti*I+t*H]*[n_A+n_B*(N-1)*p^{(\frac{\theta}{1-\theta})}]*p_A*c_{i_{AA}}$$

Each individual spends the entire wages and redistributed tariffs on products from both sectors, which originate from the home country (factor 1), foreign countries (factor I), and outside countries (factor H). We can now determine the ratio of the two consumption shares:

$$[n_A*p_A*c_{i_{AA}}+n_B*(N-1)*p_B*c_{i_{Ak}}]*[1+I+H] = w_A+T/L$$

$$w_A = [n_A+n_B*(N-1)*p^{(\frac{\theta}{1-\theta})}]*[1+(1-K*ti)*I+(1-K*t)*H]*p_A*c_{i_{AA}} \quad \text{(A-16)}$$

$$w_B = [n_A+n_B*(N-1)*p^{(\frac{\theta}{1-\theta})}]*[1+(1-K*ti)*I+(1-K*t)*H]*p_A*c_{i_{BA}}$$

$$\Leftrightarrow \quad w_A / w_B = c_{i_{AA}} / c_{i_{BA}}$$

Since labor and capital are immobile across sectors and across countries, trade must be balanced, which implies in this case that the value of the goods B purchased by all consumers A must be equal to the value of the goods A purchased by all consumers B. Budget and trade balance together then determine the relative prices, which are unchanged from our previous model:

$$N*\delta*w_A*[n_B*(N-1)*p^{(\frac{\theta}{1-\theta})}]*[1+I+H] = N*(1-\delta)*w_B*[n_A]*[1+I+H]$$

$$\Leftrightarrow \quad \frac{w_A}{w_B} = (\frac{1-\delta}{\delta})*(\frac{n_A}{n_B*(N-1)})*p^{(\frac{\theta}{\theta-1})} = 1*p^{(\frac{\theta}{\theta-1})}$$

$$\text{hence} \quad \frac{c_{i_{AA}}}{c_{i_{BA}}} = \frac{w_A}{w_B} = p^{(\frac{\theta}{\theta-1})} \quad \text{and} \quad \frac{w_A}{w_B} = \frac{p_A/(\beta-s)}{p_B/\beta} \quad \text{(A-17)}$$

$$\Leftrightarrow \quad p = \frac{p_A}{p_B} = (\frac{w_A}{w_B})^{(\frac{\theta-1}{\theta})} = (\frac{\beta-s}{\beta})^{1-\theta} < 1$$

$$\text{and} \quad \frac{w_A}{w_B} = (\frac{\beta}{\beta-s})^{\theta} > 1 \quad \text{and} \quad \frac{w_A/p_A}{w_B/p_B} = \frac{\beta}{\beta-s} > 1$$

<C> Consumption Shares Determine Value of the Utility Function and World Welfare:

Starting from the budget constraint of an individual in sector A, we replace wages, prices, and varieties with the results from the previous sections and determine one consumption share c_{iAA}:

$$c_{i_{AA}} = \frac{w_A}{p_A} \;/\; [n_A + n_B*(N-1)*p^{(\frac{\theta}{1-\theta})}] \;/\; [1+(1-K*ti)*I+(1-K*t)*H] \tag{A-18}$$

$$\Leftrightarrow \; c_{i_{AA}} = (\frac{\alpha}{\beta-s})*(\frac{\theta}{1-\theta})*\frac{1}{L}*\frac{1}{K}*\frac{1}{[1+(1-K*ti)*I+(1-K*t)*H]}$$

Again we can simplify the utility function as a function of only one consumption share, and then find the utility function for the average consumer in one country, which because of symmetry is equal to world welfare. However, we are assuming here, that the utility of each consumer is weighted equally.

$$U_A = [n_A + n_B*(N-1)*p^{(\frac{\theta}{1-\theta})}]*[1+I+H] * (c_{i_{AA}})^{\theta}$$

$$U_B = U_A * (\frac{w_B}{w_A})^{\theta} \quad and \quad U = \delta*U_A + (1-\delta)*U_B \tag{A-19}$$

$$\Leftrightarrow \; U = [\delta + (1-\delta)*(\frac{\beta-s}{\beta})^{\theta*\theta}]*(\frac{1-\theta}{\alpha})*L*K*[1+I+H] * (c_{i_{AA}})^{\theta}$$

$$U = U(\alpha,\beta,s,\delta,\theta,t,ti,g,L,N,C)$$

In addition to the closed-economy utility function, our world utility now depends on the relative size δ of the two sectors A and B, the extent of scale economies s, the number of trading blocks C in a world of N countries, and the size of tariffs (t and ti) and transport costs (g).

9. FIGURES

Figure 1: Three World Trading Blocks

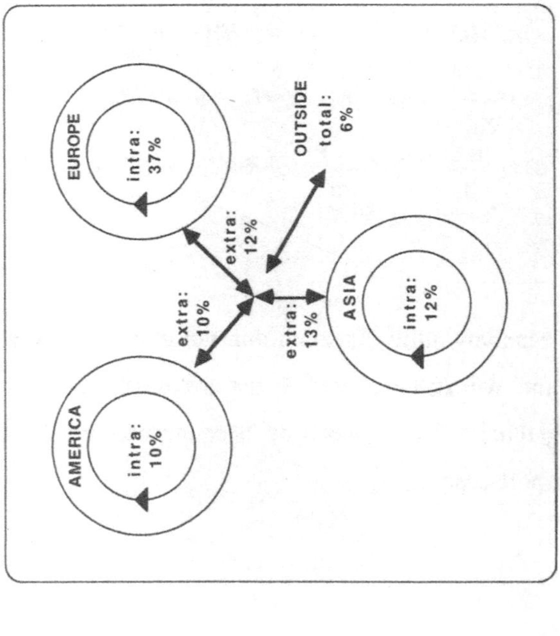

World Intra- and Extra- Regional Trade (in %, 1991):

Intra-Regional within three blocks: 59% of trade

Extra-Regional among three blocks: 35% of trade

Figure 2: Symmetrical Two-Sector-Model of International Trade

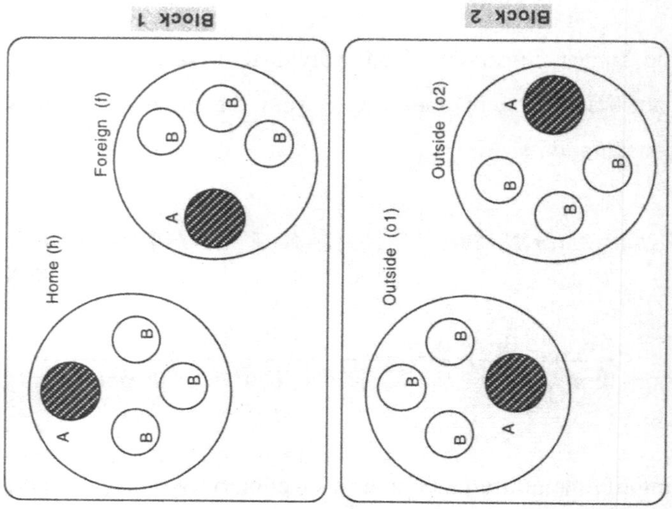

Two Sector Model with N=4 countries and C=2 Blocks

including 1 industry in sector A and (N-1) industries in sector B

Each country has absolute comparative advantage in sector A

Figure 3: Krugman's (1992) Basic Trading Block Model

one sector model (δ=0); no scale economies (s=0);
no transport cost (g=0) ; no internal tariff (ti=0):

o	upper graph:	tariff t=0.25; theta=0.80:	min welfare at C=3 blocks
Δ	middle graph:	tariff t=0.30; theta=0.75:	min welfare at C=3 blocks
◊	lower graph:	tariff t=0.25; theta=0.70:	min welfare at C=4 blocks

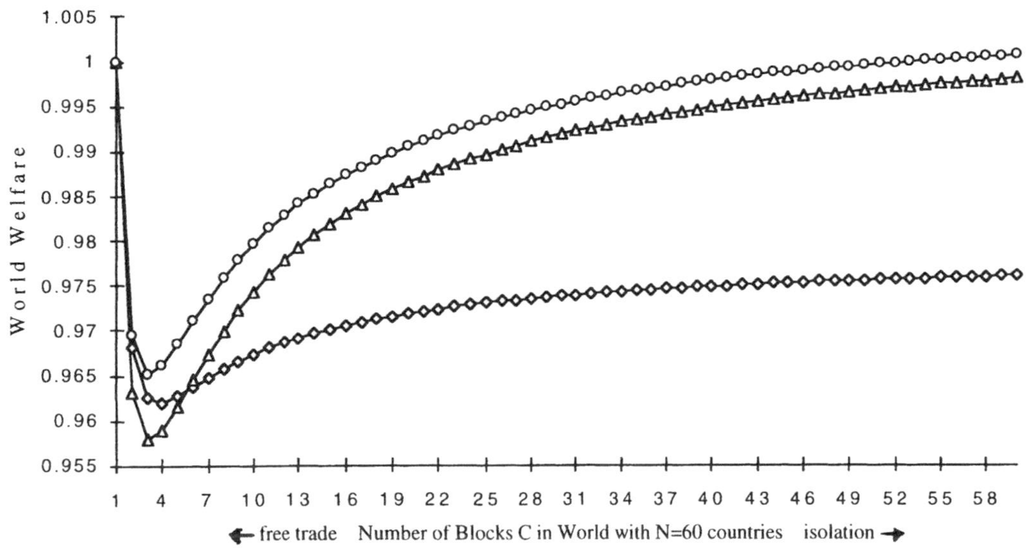

Note: world welfare under free trade for each scenario normalized to 1.

Figure 4: Two-Sector Trading Block Model with Comparative Advantage (high tariff)

two sector model (1>δ>0); existing scale economies (1>s>0);
no transport cost (g=0) ; no internal tariff (ti=0); θ=0.75:

◊	**upper graph:**	**tariff t=0.45; d=1.00; s=0.20:**	**min welfare at C=3 blocks (à la Krugman)**
Δ	**middle graph:**	**tariff t=0.45; d=0.50; s=0.40:**	**min welfare at C=5 blocks**
o	**lower graph:**	**tariff t=0.45; d=0.25; s=0.80:**	**monotonously declining welfare**

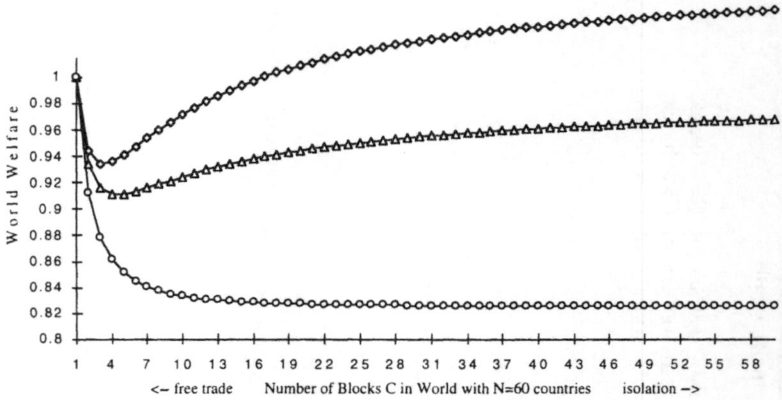

Note: world welfare under free trade for each scenario normalized to 1.

Figure 5: Two-Sector Trading Block Model with Comparative Advantage (low tariff)

two sector model (1>δ>0); existing scale economies (1>s>0);
no transport cost (g=0) ; no internal tariff (ti=0); θ=0.75:

◊	**upper graph:**	**tariff t=0.15; d=1.00; s=0.20:**	**min welfare at C=5 blocks (à la Krugman)**
Δ	**middle graph:**	**tariff t=0.15; d=0.50; s=0.40:**	**monotonously declining welfare**
o	**lower graph:**	**tariff t=0.15; d=0.25; s=0.80:**	**monotonously declining welfare**

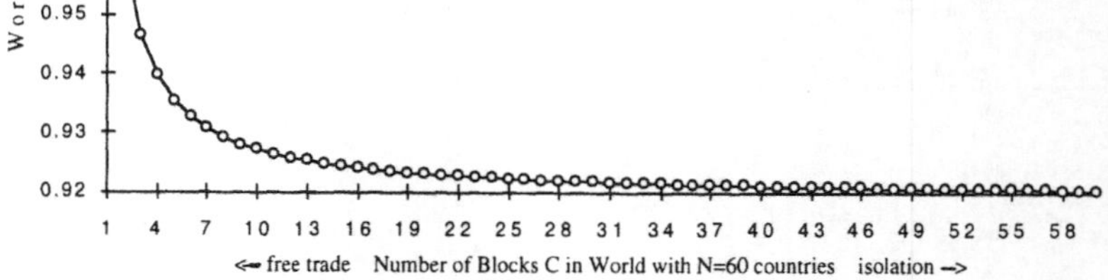

Note: world welfare under free trade for each scenario normalized to 1.

Figure 6: Two-Sector Trading Block Model with Inter-Continental Transport Costs

two sector model (1>δ>0); existing scale economies (1>s>0);
transport cost (1>g>0); no internal tariff (ti=0);
tariff rate t=0.25; transport costs g=0.20; θ=0.75:

o	upper graph:	d=0.25; s=0.80:	Max at +30%; monotonously declining welfare
Δ	middle graph:	d=0.40; s=0.50:	Max at + 7%; monotonously declining welfare
◊	lower graph:	d=1.00; s=0.20:	Max normalized to 1; min welfare at C=13 blocks

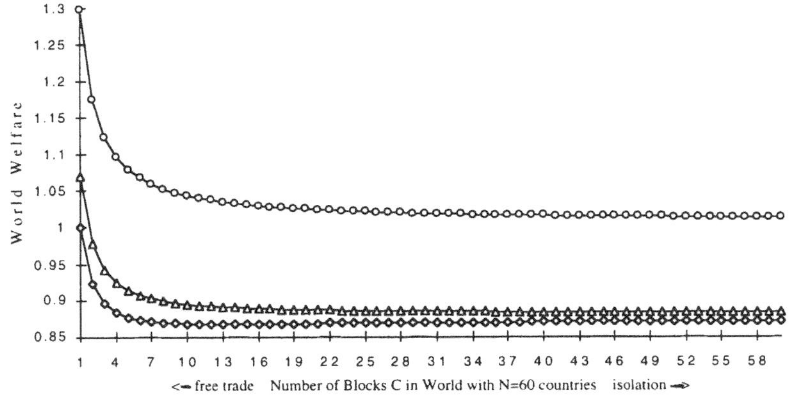

Figure 7: Two-Sector Trading Block Model with PTAs (remaining intra-block tariffs)

two sector model (1>δ>0); existing scale economies (1>s>0);
transport cost (1>g>0); intra-block tariff ti=0.05;
tariff rate t=0.25; reduced transport costs g=0.10; θ=0.75:

o	upper graph:	d=0.25; s=0.80:	Max at +27%; monotonously declining welfare
Δ	middle graph:	d=0.40; s=0.50:	Max at + 6%; monotonously declining welfare
◊	lower graph:	d=1.00; s=0.20:	Max normalized to 1; min welfare at C=7 blocks

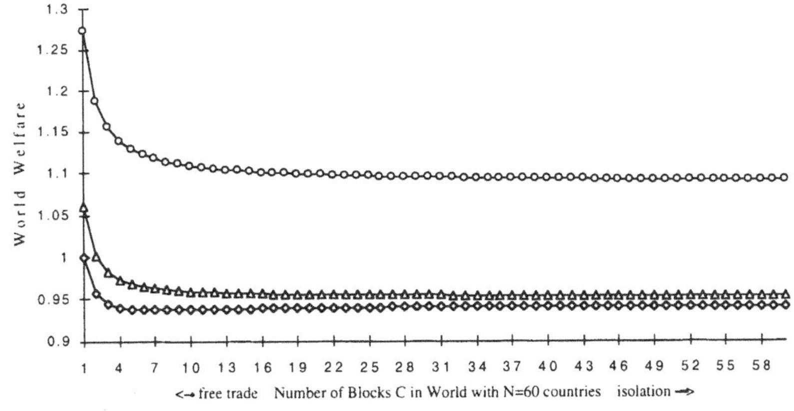

Figure 8: Parameter-Fields for Krugman (A) / Fratzscher (B) Models

	two sector trading block model ($1>\delta>0$) ; $\theta=0.75$;
	existing scale economies ($1>s>0$ and $\delta*s=0.1$) ;
lower line:	no transport cost (g=0) ; no internal tariff (ti=0).
upper line:	transport cost (g=0.10) ; internal tariff (ti=0.05).
Field A:	V-shaped utility functions (Krugman)
Field B:	L-shaped utility functions (Fratzscher)

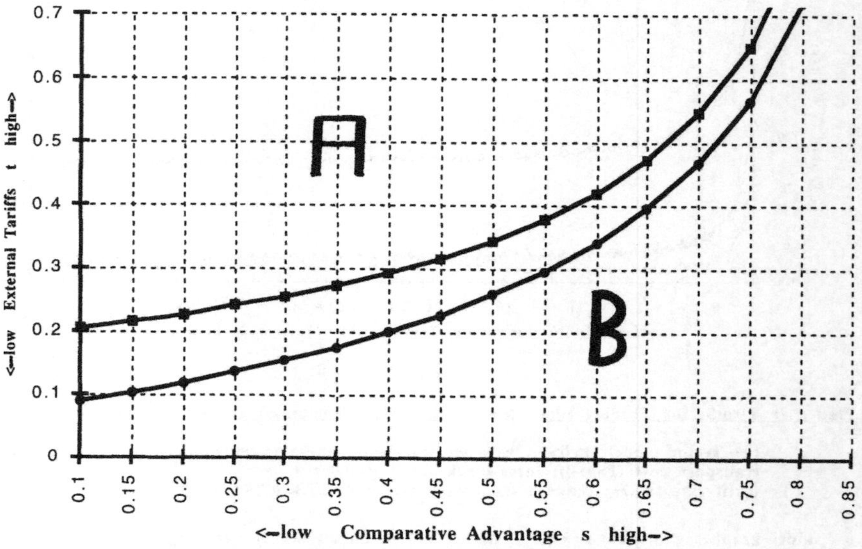

Critical tariff values t: L-shape below and V-shape above

t=0.064	no comp.advantage	s=0	ti=0	g=0	θ=0.75
t=0.118	little comp.advantage	s=0.20	ti=0	g=0	θ=0.75
t=0.199	medium comp.advantage	s=0.40	ti=0	g=0	θ=0.75
t=0.718	high comp.advantage	s=0.80	ti=0	g=0	θ=0.75
t=0.226	little comp.advantage	s=0.20	ti=0.05	g=0.10	θ=0.75
t=0.291	medium comp.advantage	s=0.40	ti=0.05	g=0.10	θ=0.75
t=0.818	high comp.advantage	s=0.80	ti=0.05	g=0.10	θ=0.75
t=0.079	medium comp.advantage	s=0.40	ti=0	g=0	θ=0.90
t=0.408	medium comp.advantage	s=0.40	ti=0	g=0	θ=0.50

Figure 9: Minimum-Utility-Values as a General Function of s and t

two sector trading block model (1>δ>0) ; θ=0.75 ;
existing scale economies (1>s>0 and δ*s=0.1) ;
no transport cost (g=0) ; no internal tariff (ti=0).

Example A: no comparative advantage (s=0) and t>0.06: MIN=3
Example B: high comparative advantage (s=0.80) and t<0.64: MIN=60
Example C: medium comp. advantage (s=0.20) and t=0.40: MIN=6

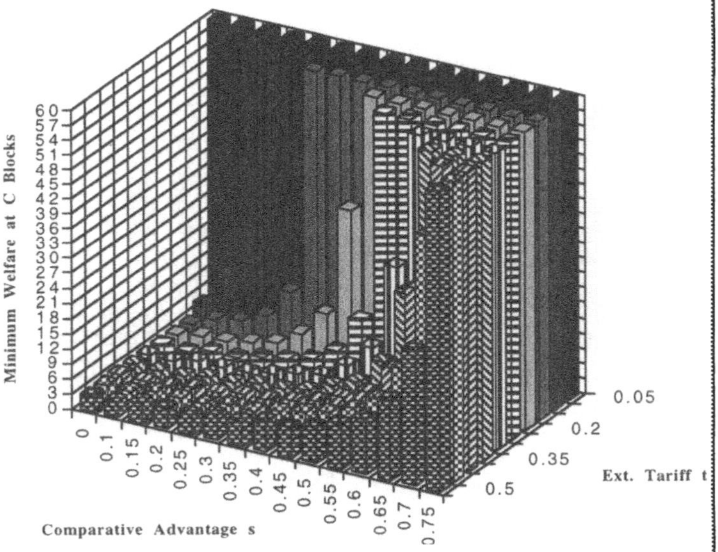

POLITICAL ECONOMY OF TRADE INTEGRATION

-- A MECHANISM OF CENTRAL EUROPEAN INTEGRATION

Abstract:

Chapter II combines a political economy model with a trading block model, where domestic interest groups lobby their government to proceed with sequential trade integration. In theory, trade integration is not politically sustainable when consumers' and producers' interests are opposed, unless a mechanism is designed which links gradual trade integration with factor reallocation and which worsens the best alternative to integration. In practice, it appears that regional integration in Central Europe implements such a mechanism, but that the eastern enlargement of the European Union is blocked by special interests of a few producers and some national governments.

Keywords: trade integration; political economy; interest groups; Central Europe; European integration; regionalism.

1. INTRODUCTION

The distribution of gains and losses from international trade both among domestic actors and among nations has obvious political significance. The implementation of a free-trade agreement requires advantages for all participating nations and also an adequate distribution of benefits among domestic interest groups. This paper shows that a mechanism of sequential trade integration can improve the political sustainability of a free-trade agreement. Two elements of that mechanism are important: first, trade integration combined with factor reallocation can help to shift domestic political interests, and second, sequencing can change the set of available alternatives.

The following section illustrates the impact of trade liberalization on domestic interest groups, and the influence of domestic interest groups on policy makers. Four interest groups are distinguished: producers in the export sector, producers in the import-substitution sector, a representative consumer, and one special interest group. A pressure group model reveals how the constituents' interests are translated via monetary or voting contributions to the policy formation process of the government. After some assumptions are specified, one main condition is derived under which in general an integration agreement is politically sustainable.

The subsequent section then extends that framework to a model of sequential trade integration. With the help of a modified trading block model, a two-period simulation illustrates that two effects are crucial to build domestic support for trade integration: in the first period, productive resources are transferred from the import-competition sector to the export sector, and in the second period, the best available alternative to integration has worsened.

These theoretical findings are then analyzed from supply and demand perspectives of European integration. It appears that the creation of the Central European Free Trade Area (CEFTA) has established a mechanism of gradual trade integration which is politically sustainable, because it enhances structural reforms and strengthens the case that all countries finally integrate into the European Union, since the alternative of isolation becomes worse. On the supply side, however, special interests of a few producers and national governments so far have blocked further enlargement. Finally, after the mechanism of trade integration has been studied from a theoretical and a more applied angle, some results are summarized and ideas for future research are presented.

2. A Pressure Group Model of Trade Policy

Previous Studies

The relationship between trade agreements and domestic politics has recently attracted renewed interest. Rogowski (1989) analyzed the structure of domestic political support for free-trade agreements and used two explanatory variables in studying the gains and losses from these agreements for domestic interest groups: the distribution of productive factors across nations and the variation in trade exposure. His theory represents a political elaboration of the Stolper-Samuelson theorem, a corollary of the factor endowments theory of international trade. According to the *factor endowments theory*, a country exports those goods which are produced by productive factors which the country possesses in relative abundance. According to the *Stolper-Samuelson theorem*, increased trade exposure adversely affects domestic owners of relatively scarce productive factors and benefits those owning relatively abundant factors.[1/]

Rogowski combined these two theorems of trade with a simple model of politics and was able to predict political coalitions reflecting the preferences of domestic owners of productive factors. He pointed out that beneficiaries of changing trade exposure want to accelerate changes, and that these actors who enjoy a sudden increase in wealth or income are able to overcome collective action obstacles and exercise expanded political influence. Midford (1993) extended Rogowski's three-factor framework and included eleven productive factors, as proposed in Leamer's (1984) factor endowments model. That extended framework illustrates even more clearly the divided interests among domestic interest groups.

1/ That theorem was originally presented in Stolper and Samuelson (1941), and is also illustrated in Ethier (1988, pp 100-109).

In the following, we attempt to illustrate these insights in a more formal political economy model. First, the domestic interest groups are characterized and their potential gains and losses from trade liberalization are analyzed. Then, a pressure group model is elaborated which translates these economic interests into political power. We illustrate the functioning of that pressure group model in a world of trading blocks, which enables us to study the effects of sequential trade integration. That theoretical analysis reveals a necessary condition for a politically sustainable path of integration and identifies four key variables. Finally, those theoretical insights are translated into the context of Central European integration.

Domestic Interest Groups

We distinguish four domestic interest groups: A) producers typically supporting liberalization such as exporters, B) producers typically loosing from liberalization such as import-substitution industries, C) consumers, and D) a final special-interest group typically guided more by ideological than economic views on trade policy. We assume for simplicity that the interests of these four groups are independent and can be added in a linear function. Moreover, producers' interests are only guided by profits, while consumers' interests are formed only by their utility from consumption. It is also assumed that all productive factors are domestically owned and that all individuals' interests within one sector are identical.

We now study the implications of trade integration on these four domestic interest groups and focus the analysis on one particular arrangement of trade integration, namely free-trade areas. According to article XXIV of the GATT agreement, countries can form a free-trade area if they eliminate or substantially reduce duties and other regulations of commerce on substantially all trade among themselves. We assume that countries within the free-trade area retain a common external tariff (t) on trade with the rest of the world, but reduce the internal tariff ($ti < t$) on trade conducted between them. Moreover, it is possible that for some transitional period, a few politically sensitive sectors are excluded from that tariff reduction so that both internal and external tariffs remain at t. Welfare implications now crucially depend on two assumptions, namely on the production function and the structure of factor endowments.

Implications from Trade Integration

In a world where *production* exhibits constant returns to scale, benefits from integration are usually limited, and only lead to a slightly increased utility of consumers through the improved access to a larger variety of products, whereas the effect of integration on prices is often negligible. On the other hand, in a world of differentiated products with increasing returns to scale, integration usually leads to enhanced specialization and reduced production costs, which lead to higher profits of producers and higher incomes of consumers. Usually, the benefits of integration for producers are uneven, with exporters getting most benefits through an improved access to foreign markets, while importers usually benefit only through higher demand by domestic consumers. Moreover, changing prices can also alter the terms-of-trade.

In a world where *factor endowments* differ substantially across free-trade areas, we often observe that trade integration leads to enhanced protection, since producers intend to maintain higher domestic prices and hence higher profits. That is possible, if countries of a free-trade area import a substantial share of one product from the rest of the world, so that prices for that product remain at (1+t). Despite the reduced internal tariffs, the internal trade in that product will also be conducted at the same price of (1+t), so that producers gain the benefits of the reduced tariffs while governments loose the same amount in tariff revenue. In the opposite case, where factor endowments are very similar across free-trade areas, internal demand of that product can be satisfied by internal production, and trade is conducted at lower prices of (1+ti), which implies higher benefits for consumers, but less profits for producers.

What picture do we observe in reality? In industrialized countries, we observe a large degree of trade in differentiated products and usually increasing returns in production. Moreover, trade integration usually leads to declining internal tariffs and declining prices, assuming that trading blocks are formed among natural partners. Interests of the four domestic interest groups are often opposed: Exporters usually gain through reduced tariffs, increasing returns to scale, and improved market access, but a reduction in prices may offset some gains. Import-substituting industries usually loose most from integration, especially if the initial protection had been high and producer prices drop significantly. Consumers usually gain through higher wages, a larger variety of products, and lower prices, but reduced tariff revenues[2/] may offset some gains. Furthermore, all interest groups may achieve additional gains through higher investment and growth (Baldwin, 1989) or through higher wages and higher employment (Krugman and Lawrence, 1994).

Particular attention should be paid to interests of the fourth special interest group. We often observe strong ideological resistance to trade liberalization in certain political circles. That resistance is often ideological, it may be motivated by historical developments, or arise through current political or structural changes. For instance, trade can create political dependencies (as we observed in the former Comecon block and in the managed trade during the 1930s), trade can reduce the self-sufficiency of countries (as for instance revealed by the sharp decline of steel production in some European countries), and trade can induce structural changes with substantial adjustment costs (as for instance experienced in the Southern European integration). Most likely, these non-economic interests are stronger in countries which have experienced high protection, which have employed a large proportion of their labor force in less competitive industries, and which experienced some failure of regional integration in the past.

2/ We assume that tariff revenue is collected by the government and then redistributed as a lump-sum transfer to consumers, so that the formation of a free-trade area implies lower transfers to consumers.

Political Transmission Mechanism

How are the interests of these four domestic interests groups transmitted into the decision process of policy makers? Two categories of models have been developed to answer that question:[3/] first, the *median-voter-model* (e.g. Mayer, 1984) assumes that government policies are determined by the interests of the median voter, but in reality we often observe large gaps between the position of governments and the interests of their constituents, especially when long-term decisions on trade policy are made. Second, the *pressure-group-model*, developed by Olson (1965) and recently refined by Grossman and Helpman (1994), assumes that the government is not simply a mouthpiece for the people, but its decisions are strongly influenced by lobbying activities.

Hillman (1989) and Baldwin (1985) pointed out why lobbying activities are so important. They observed that many constituents are not aware of all government policies and their economic consequences, and that elected officials are often not fully aware of the economic interests of their electorate. Therefore, they suggested that voters, either producers or consumers, may have to engage in costly lobbying activities to bring their interests to the attention of legislators. Moreover, politicians may need funds to inform their voters on how well they have served them in order to ensure reelection.

3/ This part draws on the analysis of Baldwin (1993).

A Pressure Group Model

In the following, we present a general form of a pressure-group-model which is similar to that presented by Grossman and Helpman (1994), and based on two crucial assumptions: First, the policy maker's objective function is linear in campaign donations of producers, in overall social welfare of consumers, and also takes account of ideological resistance of special interest groups. The fixed-weight linear objective function expresses the politicians' chances for reelection, which increase linearly in aggregate campaign contributions, utilities of individual voters, and declining ideological resistance of special interest groups. Second, interest groups can specify donation contracts contingent on the actions of the policy maker in the following way: Interests groups announce in the first of two periods, how large donations will be for each possible policy stance, and in the second period, the government sets the optimal policy and collects the donations.

Given the linear objective function and the contingent donation contracts, the political process can be framed as a principle-agent problem, where the government acts as the agent and the interest groups as principles. That enables us to draw on a more general principal-agent theory which was developed by Bernheim and Whinston (1986a, 1986b). Grossman and Helpman (1994) simplified that problem in two steps: First, they assumed that an equilibrium exists and considered the donation contracts differentiable around that equilibrium. Second, they focused on the Bernheim-Whinston notion of a *truthful Nash equilibrium,* which restricts the contracts to a very specific form, where principles pay the agent the full marginal product minus some optimal fixed amount. Bernheim and Whinston (1986a, 1986b) defended that concept in showing that such contracts are never sub-optimal and equilibria are stable.

Following that approach by Grossman and Helpman (1994), we specify the *objective function* of the government: it can choose between two options, either to integrate or to stay outside, which is captured by a binary variable z, which equals unity if the government decides to integrate and zero in the opposite case. The fully rational government chooses z in order to maximize political support, which depends positively on campaign contributions by producers A and B, on the level of social welfare C net of donations, and on the resistance of special-interest group D. The weights are chosen as (1-y), y, and 1 respectively, which leads to the following objective function F:

$$\begin{aligned} F &= z*[(1-y)*(U_A^{in}+U_B^{in})+y*U_C^{in}] \\ &+ (1-z)*[(1-y)*(U_A^{out}+U_B^{out})+y*U_C^{out}+U_D] \qquad (1) \\ & z=1 \ [\textit{inside}] \ or \ z=0 \ [\textit{outside}] \ ; \ y\in[0,1] \end{aligned}$$

The variables U express the utilities derived from the contributions of producers A and B, from the welfare of consumers C, and from the non-resistance of special-interest groups D[4/], for the policy choice of integrating "inside" (z=1) or staying "outside" (z=0). The political distortion, or difference between consumers' interest and government policy, is expressed by parameter

---

4/ U_D is measured positively, indicating the utility derived from the non-resistance in the policy choice z=0. In the opposite case, the government may take the risk of provoking large protests, disruptions, strikes, etc.

y, which can range from zero to one. At unity, the government acts to maximize social welfare, and when y gets close to zero, exporters' interests become dominant in the formation of governmental policy.

Following Grossman and Helpman (1994), *donation contracts* are restricted to be truthful in the Bernheim-Whinston notion, which implies that they are non-negative and that each interest group lobbies for only one policy. Consequently, contributions of A for "out" are zero, contributions of B for "in" are zero, and support (non-resistance) of D for "in" is zero. All producers are organized into lobbying groups (A and B) and overcome collective action problems. Their truthful donation contracts only depend on expected differences in profits:

$$\begin{aligned} U_A^{in} &= \Delta\Pi_A^{(in-out)} - const \\ U_B^{out} &= \Delta\Pi_B^{(out-in)} - const \end{aligned} \tag{2}$$

Given these donation contracts, what is a *necessary condition* for integration? A fully rational government decides to integrate (z=1) if and only if the resistance of D (left side) is smaller or equal than the weighted sum of the difference in contributions supporting integration (right side, first term) and the difference in social welfare from integration (second term):

$$z = 1 \ (ie.\,integration) \quad if\ and\ only\ if:$$

$$U_D^{out} \le (1-y)*[\Delta\Pi_A^{(in-out)} - \Delta\Pi_B^{(out-in)}] + y*[\Delta U_C^{(in-out)}] \tag{3}$$

$$z = z(\Delta\Pi_A^{(+)}; \Delta\Pi_B^{(-)}; \Delta U_C^{(+)}; U_D^{(-)}) \qquad y \in [0,1]$$

The political choice of producers under truthful donation contracts is limited to the size of the constant term. That term is determined by the voluntary participation constraint, meaning that the producers choose a level where the government is at least indifferent to accepting their donation contract. Grossman and Helpman (1994) demonstrated much more in detail the algebra and also derived a more general solution without using the participation constraint.

As we can see in equation 3, the government's policy choice only depends on *four variables*: the expected differences in profits of exporters, the expected differences in profits of import-substitution industries, the expected difference in social welfare, and the expected resistance of special interest groups.

Grossman and Helpman (1993) studied the effects of these variables in some generality: They argued that governments are more likely to reject trade integration ($z=0$) in one of the following three cases: First, if initial protection is very high, the expected decline in profits of import-substituting industries is higher and so is the political cost. Second, if initially trade deficits are large, the chances of exporters to benefit from integration are smaller, and hence political support is lower. Third, if integration occurs on a very small scale among countries with very different factor endowments, enhanced protection is more likely, prices decline less than they could in a larger integration agreement, and the benefits for consumers are smaller.

However, the fourth variable has not been mentioned in their study. The success of trade integration may depend on country-specific factors. Trade integration would more likely be rejected (z=0) in one of the following three cases: First, if the country in question is of medium size (eg. France), it does not vitally depend on trade integration like very small countries do (eg. Belgium), and it does not risk to loose its leadership role in multilateral negotiations like very large countries do (eg. United States), so that a medium-sized country may more likely resist trade integration (mentioned by Lawrence, 1994). Second, if integration requires a substantial reallocation of resources, costs through temporary unemployment are high and political support erodes. Third, if the country in question had a negative historical experience with integration, such as in Comecon countries where trade dependencies were imposed, the psychological resistance to integration tends to be higher.

To summarize our insights from this theoretical part, we recognize that the pressure group model illustrates in a simplified principal-agent framework how domestic interest groups influence the government on policy issues (such as trade integration) with electoral votes and campaign contributions. We identified four domestic interest groups and four corresponding variables which form the government's policy choice. One necessary condition for trade integration to occur showed the typically opposed interests between producers and consumers. While producers typically lobby for enhanced protection in order to skim the benefits of remaining high tariffs, consumers prefer reduced protection since lower tariffs and prices improve the available variety of products and the value of their utility function. Hirschman (1981) already developed this argument, and Grossman and Helpman (1993, p. 27) summarized that finding as:

> *"a free-trade area is most likely to be politically viable exactly when it would be socially harmful."*

The main contribution of this paper is the linkage between a political economy framework and a more detailed trade integration model. The main question is no longer, whether trade integration *per se* is politically sustainable, but whether *gradual, sequenced* trade integration (modeled in a trading block framework) is politically preferable.

3. Simulations with a Modified Trading Block Model

This section now combines the political economy framework with a two-period trade integration model. The analysis is guided by three main questions: First, what are the conflicts of interest in the trade policy context of our political economy model? Second, how can a mechanism of trade integration be designed in order to improve political sustainability? Finally, under which conditions is a two-period gradual process of trade integration politically preferable to a one-step rapid integration? For tractability, we need to make some crucial assumptions in our model, such as strong symmetry across countries, complete domestic ownership of productive resources, and complete information of rational actors. The following two sections, therefore, will translate our findings in the context of Central European integration, and those assumptions will be critically examined.

Previous Work on Political Sustainability

Grossman and Helpman (1993) provided a very thorough political economy framework for the analysis of trade policy. However, their one-period static model does not allow to differentiate different stages of integration. On the other hand, a lot of interesting studies have been completed in recent years on the question of a gradualist versus big-bang approach, especially in the context of Central European privatization, monetary and exchange rate policy, and also price and trade liberalization. While supporters of radical reform mainly refer to efficiency and credibility arguments, advocates of a more gradual path often refer to the cost of social adjustment and the need for political sustainability. Rodrik (1992), for instance, concluded that the success of reforms is as much determined by the understanding of the underlying political economy forces as by the reform package itself. Wei (1993) traced that wisdom back to Confucius, who is quoted as having said *"more haste, less result"*.[5]

Three studies in particular have advanced the research in the field linking political sustainability and trade liberalization: Grossman and Helpman (1993)

---

[5] quoted in Wei (1993, page 1): "Yu se ze bu da" - "More haste, less result" from: *Lunyu (The Analects of Confucius) - chapter on Zhi Lu.*

elaborated a variety of necessary conditions for a free-trade agreement to be politically sustainable. Fernandez and Rodrik (1991) distinguished ex-ante and ex-post political sustainability and stressed that one key challenge of reforms is to mobilize additional political support during the implementation stage. Wei (1993) advanced that idea in modeling trade reform and concluded that rapid liberalization is more efficient whereas gradual liberalization is politically more sustainable.

This paper continues that line of research and analyzes the political sustainability of trade integration in a trading bock model. The initial motivation came from one recent policy question: Should Central European economies integrate rapidly with the European Union and the world economy at large, or should they choose a more gradual path of integration and first form a regional trading block? To some extend, actual events have answered that question, after four Central European countries signed the Central European Free Trade Agreement (CEFTA) in December 1992, which is expected to act as a catalyst for the integration of these countries into the European Union. While that decision was largely motivated by foreign policy arguments, our analysis argues that political economy reasons offer additional support for it.

Trading Block Framework

In a previous paper, I have elaborated a trading block model, which studies trade and welfare effects from sequential trade integration into growing trading blocks. The framework is derived from a trade model under monopolistic competition by Krugman (1980), based on the Dixit-Stiglitz framework (1977). The market structure is of Chamberlinian monopolistic competition, where trade is only driven by the taste for a variety of differentiated products. Krugman's original trading block model (1991a) has been extended to include two elements of comparative advantage by introducing lower marginal costs into one industry's production function and by allowing a higher share of labor being utilized in that industry. In our model, we define a world consisting of a large number of countries N, grouped into a number of symmetric trading blocks C, which each consist of N/C countries. Each country consists of N industries, which are grouped into two sectors, so that sector A (advanced) contains only the one industry which exhibits comparative advantage in production and which employs a share of δ of the labor force, and sector B (backward) contains the other (N-1) industries with normal production functions and equal labor shares. Our main result indicates that in the presence of comparative advantage, sequential trade integration monotonically improves world welfare.

For the present purpose of connecting a political economy framework to a trading block model, we need to refine our modelling to include two sectors, where trade integration can shift resources across sectors and hence change the level of political support, and where profits are modelled as potential lobbying contributions which producers may spend to influence the governments' policy. Therefore, we modify our trading block model, which was in detail elaborated in the preceding chapter, in three ways: by allowing labor mobility, by relaxing one symmetry constraint, and by modeling profits more in detail: First, we allow labor mobility from sector B to sector A which occurs during the structural adjustment process which is induced by trade integration. However, in our model we assume full employment and have labor as the only factor of production, so that we cannot model adjustment costs. Therefore, complete specialization in sector A could occur immediately, which we avoid by limiting labor mobility to the extent that after trade integration the home market share of sector A remains constant (which ceteris paribus would decline after integration) while the foreign market share rises to its equilibrium level. Moreover, we assume that the stock of modern technology and/or capital (revealed in the parameter $s^*\delta$ of the cost function) remains constant (as developed in part 4 of chapter 1).

Second, we relax one symmetry condition and allow for the possibility that individual countries can be isolated from the world economy and hence do not take part in symmetrical trade integration. We would expect that a fully isolated country experiences a higher level of protection and also reduced employment. In our trading block model, we assume that the isolation of a single country has negligible welfare implications on all other countries, but that the welfare of the outside country is determined in a model of increased protection (C=N) and reduced employment (L=0.90).[6]

Third, in order to link the trading block model with the political economy framework, we need to model producers' and consumers' interests more in detail. Here we assume that all productive resources are domestically owned, that all actors are rational in maximizing their utility and that they possess complete information. However, as pointed out above, we cannot model adjustment costs which occur when labor moves across sectors (such as retraining, sunk costs, new investment in infrastructure etc.). Intuition tells us that foreign capital inflows (not included in our model) often facilitate structural adjustment and the transition of labor, which we could only capture in our model through increased values of $s^*\delta$ in the cost function. Moreover, we disaggregate consumers' revenue into two parts, namely neo-classical wages which are equal to the workers' marginal product, and net profits which are fully redistributed to the owners (which in our model are consumers). We assume that producers (invisible in our trading block model) want to maximize operating profits,[7] which can be transformed into

---

6/ This assumption is difficult since some protectionism *can* increase national welfare. However, full scale isolation (for instance of Iraq after the Gulf War) usually implies substantial welfare losses, which in our model are best captured by lower employment. The modelling here is rather simple and intuitive, since isolation in our analysis is a very special case, which is not crucial to the argument. A more detailed asymmetric model was elaborated by Bond and Syropoulos (1993).

7/ We choose operating profits instead of net profits as the producers' objective, assuming a shorter time horizon where fixed and sunk costs are insignificant and where taxes on profits are neglected. Moreover, we look at the

campaign contributions for the government, whereas consumers want to maximize social welfare, which can be translated into electoral votes.

The following analysis elaborates some insights for our three main questions. We start by looking at the interests of the different interest groups (consumers and producers in the export and import-substitution sectors), before studying conditions for a politically sustainable trade integration, and finally analyzing whether gradual or rapid trade integration is politically more sustainable. The analysis is guided by six propositions which are based on theoretical work which is in detail presented in appendix-I.

Consumers' Interests

For the first proposition we need to recall the function of social welfare (U) from the above outlined trading block model. As known from chapter I, which derived in detail the trading block model, sequential trade integration into a smaller number C of larger trading blocks improves world welfare U in the presence of comparative advantage ($0<s<1$; $0<\delta<1$) and average tariff rates (see also figure 1a). Higher comparative advantage (larger s and δ) and higher productive resources (L) improve overall utility, while higher costs (α and β) and higher taxes (t and ti) and higher transaction costs (g) decrease overall utility.

---

aggregate of producers' operating profits (in sectors A and B) since those are most relevant to determine aggregate campaign contributions. However, given labor mobility and the entry of new firms, operating profits per plant or per worker can change. Consumers maximize their utility function and not their revenues, since they also value the consumption of a large variety of products.

$$U = [\delta + (1-\delta) * (\frac{\beta - s}{\beta})^{\theta * \theta}] * (\frac{1-\theta}{\alpha}) * L * K * [1 + I + H]$$
$$* [(\frac{\alpha}{\beta - s}) * (\frac{\theta}{1-\theta}) * \frac{1}{L} * \frac{1}{K} * \frac{1}{1+(1-K*ti)*I+(1-K*t)*H}]^{\theta} \tag{4}$$
$$U = U (\alpha^{(-)}, \beta^{(-)}, s^{(+)}, \delta^{(+)}, \theta^{(-)}, t^{(-)}, ti^{(-)}, g^{(-)}, L^{(+)}, C^{(-)})$$

Producers' Interests

Moreover, we need to calculate the overall operating profits for sector A (employing δ*L workers) and sector B (employing (1-δ)*L workers). Operating profits are defined as the volume of sales times the difference between sales price and variable costs. Profits in sectors A and B only differ because of the different labor share and the different cost functions. Details are provided in appendix-I. Obviously, operating profits increase for each additional worker in the sector (larger L and larger share of δ or (1-δ) respectively). Moreover, profits decline when costs increase (larger β or smaller s) and when transaction costs increase (larger g). However, the effect of trade integration (smaller C) and reduced tariffs (smaller t and ti) on profits is less obvious: *profits decline with more integration and lower tariffs.*[8/] In the absence of price changes (no terms-of-trade effects) and of factor mobility (constant δ and s), trade integration implies

---

8/ Both derivatives are negative for a realistic range of parameters. Analytical solutions are getting very complicated, so that numerical calculations of derivatives are used. First, in the presence of some comparative advantage (s=0.4 and δ=0.25) and average tariff rates (t=0.15 and ti=0 or t=0.25 and ti=0.05), trade integration (lower C) decreases producer profits (see figure 1b). Second, in the presence of some comparative advantage and external tariffs and transaction costs (t=0.25 and ti=0.05 and g=0.10), an increase in external tariff rates increases producer profits (see figure 1c).

for the producer that less products are sold in the domestic market (because of more foreign competition) and more products are sold in the foreign market (because of lower tariffs). If a producer now sells one car less at home and instead one car more abroad at the same price, the profits decline because of the positive transaction costs g. Only when the scale effects, which occur when labor can switch from sector B to sector A,[9] allow production costs to decline, will overall profits after trade integration improve. Our main result here is that although long-term profits from trade integration *with* factor mobility will increase, these profits will decrease when trade integration occurs *without* factor mobility.

$$\pi_A = \delta * L * w_A * (1-\theta) * \left[\frac{1+I+H}{1+(1-K*ti)*I+(1-K*t)*H}\right]$$
$$\pi_B = \pi_A * \left(\frac{\beta - s}{\beta}\right)^{\theta} * \left(\frac{1-\delta}{\delta}\right) \qquad (5)$$
$$\pi_A = \pi_A\,(\,\beta^{(+)}, s^{(-)}, \delta^{(+)}, \theta^{(-)}, t^{(+)}, ti^{(+)}, g^{(-)}, C^{(+)}, L^{(+)}\,)$$
$$\pi_B = \pi_B\,(\,\beta^{(+)}, s^{(-)}, \delta^{(-)}, \theta^{(-)}, t^{(+)}, ti^{(+)}, g^{(-)}, C^{(+)}, L^{(+)}\,)$$

Interests of producers in sectors A and B only diverge regarding factor reallocation (δ): since production in sector A is more efficient, labor will be reallocated from sector B into sector A, so that profits of sector B as a whole (not necessarily of the individual firm) will decline, whereas profits of sector A will increase. In other words, in the presence of fixed and fully employed productive

---

9/ Indeed there may be some reallocation of labor within each sector, but in our model that effect is not strong enough to produce scale effects large enough to balance the additional transaction costs.

resources, factor reallocation implies profit reallocation across sectors. Moreover, interests of producers and consumers regarding trade integration (pure) are generally opposed: while consumers gain from the availability of a larger variety of products, producers lose from the increased transaction costs. However, interests of producers change once trade integration (lower C) *and* labor reallocation (higher δ) are implemented simultaneously: while consumers and producers in sector A gain, producers in sector B loose. Table 1 (page 20) illustrates these effects for two numerical examples.

Proposition 1: Interests of producers and consumers regarding trade integration (lower C) are generally opposed: consumers gain and producers loose. However, interests of consumers and producers in sector A coincide once trade integration *and* labor reallocation occur simultaneously: consumers and producers in sector A gain, whereas producers in sector B loose.

The derivatives are shown below and also illustrated in figure 1 for some sets of parameters: Figure 1a shows that $\delta U/\delta C<0$ in a wide range of parameters, unless very little or no comparative advantage is present (d=1) or tariff rates are much above average (t>0.30). Figure 1b shows that $\delta\pi/\delta C>0$ in a wide range of parameters, unless all tariffs are zero, or internal tariffs exceed external tariffs (ti>=t) or there is little preference for variety ($\Theta>0.90$).

$$\frac{\delta U}{\delta C} < 0 \; ; \; \frac{\delta \pi_A}{\delta C} > 0 \; ; \; \frac{\delta \pi_B}{\delta C} > 0$$
$$\frac{\delta U}{\delta \delta} > 0 \; ; \; \frac{\delta \pi_A}{\delta \delta} > 0 \; ; \; \frac{\delta \pi_B}{\delta \delta} < 0 \qquad (6)$$

Figure 1: Partial Derivatives of Social Welfare U and Profits π_A

Partial Derivative d(social welfare U) / d(number of trading blocks C)

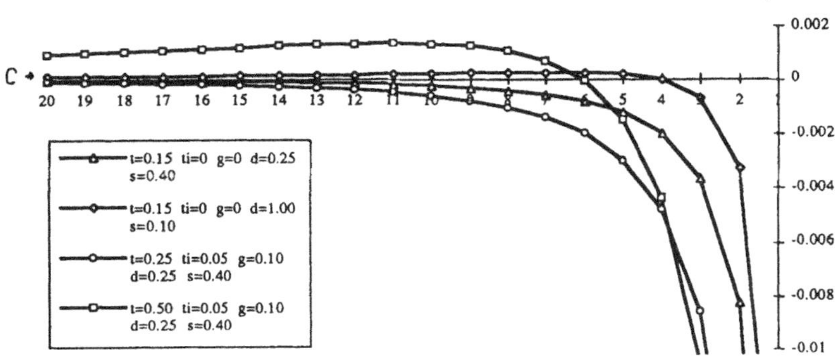

Partial Derivative d(profits sector A) / d(number of trading blocks C)

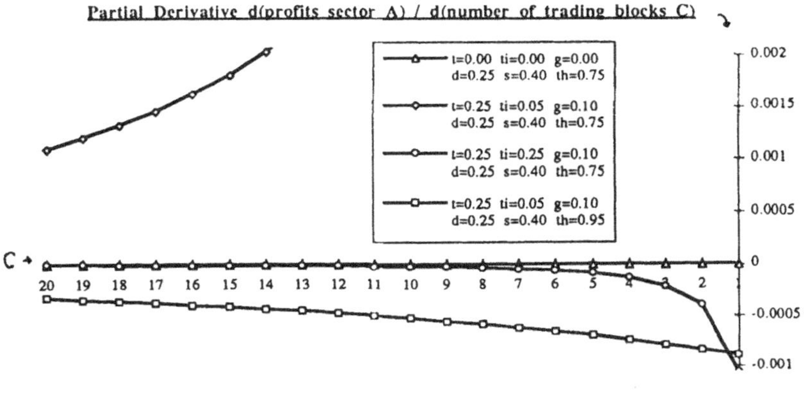

Partial Derivative d(profits sector A) / d(external tariffs t)

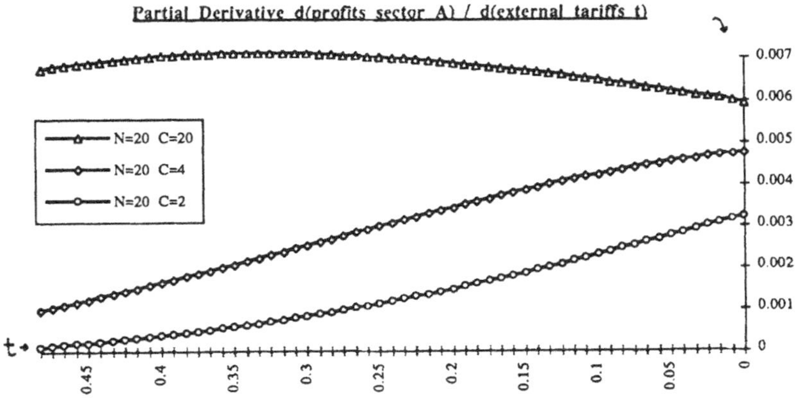

Exporters Versus Importers

We have now distinguished between consumers' and producers' interests, but have not yet clarified the relationship between producers in our trading block model and the export-industry and import-substitution industry in our political economy model. In reality, very rarely producers exclusively produce only for the domestic market or only for the export market, there nearly always is some combination of both and that is also the case in our trading block model. In a world where differentiated products are present, each firm produces a unique product, and consumers benefit from trade because they obtain access to a larger variety of products. Consumers hence purchase products A and B both from domestic producers and from foreign producers, so that in each sector, products are being imported and are being exported.

The net trade balance in each sector is determined by two effects: first, a large share of labor (δ*L) creates a so-called home-market-effect (Krugman, 1980) which leads through scale economies to a larger volume of exports. Second, a more efficient and cheaper production (eg. higher parameter s in cost function) leads through improved productivity again to a higher volume of exports. Finally, in a world with immobile capital, trade between countries and between sectors must be balanced, which implies that the net trade surplus of one sector must be equal to the net trade deficit in the other sector.

Hence, in our model there are no export and import-competition sectors per se, but sectors A and B represent similar interests: one sector has positive net exports while the other one has the mirror positive net imports. It turns out that the home-market-effect is dominant in our model. If we assume that sector B employs 75% of the labor force and sector A reveals a cost-advantage of 40% (structure (i) of table 1), then sector B shows positive net exports. Only when the labor share approaches 50%, the structure changes and sector A shows positive net exports, while sector B has shifted to positive net imports. That change is often the effect of trade integration and labor reallocation: prior to integration, the backward sector B employs most of the labor force and shows positive net exports, whereas after integration and labor reallocation, the advanced sector has shifted to become a net exporter. Therefore, for the purpose of our political economy model, sector A represents typical export-sector interests, and sector B represents typical import-competition-sector interests.

Proposition 2: Originally, sector B may be a net exporter, but after integration and labor reallocation, sector A acquires a higher proportion of labor because of its higher productivity and hence sector A becomes a net exporter, while sector B shows net imports.

Rapid Versus Gradual Integration

Table 1 illustrates in row <1> an example which shows that rapid trade integration is often politically unsustainable, because producer losses are becoming very large. Unless the government is strongly biased towards consumers' interests, it would not implement rapid trade integration in the presence of large losses imposed on producers, since its revenue from producers' contributions would be lower than optimal. That assessment changes, of course, once factor mobility occurs - once labor is reallocated across sectors, the combined effects from trade integration and factor reallocation become positive for producers in sector A and for consumers. Although rapid trade integration may be preferable from an efficient point of view, it appears that it is often not politically sustainable.

Proposition 3: Rapid integration is politically often not sustainable.

Role of Initial Conditions

Apparently, support for trade integration differs among similar countries. Although we have included a fourth domestic interest group guided by non-economic motives in our model, it is very likely that initial structural conditions may also be different. Intuitively, it appears that high initial protection hinders integration, since a large decline in protection implies larger producer losses. Indeed, we derive a positive partial derivative of producer profits and external tariffs (figure 1c), meaning that producers in both sectors prefer higher protection. On the other hand, consumers loose through higher protection since the available variety of products is reduced.

Moreover, the larger the initial size of sector A, and the larger the initial comparative advantage in the economy, the better will be the chances to politically sustain trade integration. First, a larger sector A implies the presence of more potential supporters. Second, higher comparative advantage implies more consumers' benefits from trade integration and avoids a V-shaped social welfare function (figure 1a), where consumers would loose in the initial stages.

Proposition 4: Low initial protection improves political support for integration, since producers' losses are smaller. Large comparative advantage improves political support for integration, since consumers benefit from a larger variety and avoid losses in initial stages.

The partial derivatives are found numerically as illustrated in figure 1:

$$\frac{\delta U}{\delta t} < 0 \; ; \; \frac{\delta \pi_A}{\delta t} > 0 \; ; \; \frac{\delta \pi_B}{\delta t} > 0 \tag{7}$$

Mechanism Design to Improve Political Sustainability

Gradual integration provides more time for implementing trade policies leading towards integration. That additional time allows two structural changes to take place which may improve the design in order to become more politically sustainable: First, support for the reforms may increase if labor is reallocated from sector B to sector A. That idea was recently elaborated by Wei (1993) and Dewatripont and Roland (1993). Second, opposition against reforms may decrease if the best available alternative worsens, for instance if the country becomes isolated. That idea was elaborated by Baldwin (1993) and also recently discussed in the context of integrating four EFTA countries into the European Union. Both structural changes are present in our model: labor shifts from sector B to sector A, and after a first round of regional integration, the alternative to full integration becomes isolation.

The first element of improving the mechanism design is to improve political support: While rapid trade integration can be implemented relatively fast, it cannot build ex-ante on a growing export sector, since labor reallocation needs additional time. On the other hand, gradual trade integration usually combines trade policy reforms with structural reforms, so that after the initial first step of integration some labor is reallocated, and the extended base of support is available ex-ante for the second step of integration.

Table 1 illustrates that process for a world with 20 countries, which first integrate into four regions, and then into a world of free trade. As shown in row <2>, the first step of integration from 20 to 4 implies welfare gains for consumers, and welfare losses for producers in both sectors, which are relatively small (less than half of the size) compared to those of rapid integration shown in row <1>. The following structural change reallocates 15% of the labor force from sector B into sector A, implying a substantial increase of profits in the enlarged sector A, which by far exceeds the additional losses sustained by sector

B. In other words, support among producers on average is rising and so are their campaign contributions to the government. However, that mechanism is based on a critical but often realistic assumption, namely the myopia by producers, where nobody knows who out of sector B will be able to transfer into sector A.

The same reasoning holds for the second step of integration. However, full integration into a world of free trade implies a more substantial reallocation of labor, so that the costs for sector B are getting substantially larger (-6.73 compared to -0.49). On the other hand, the main benefits for consumers are realized in this final stage of integration. Hence we would expect that interests become more polarized in the final step of integration, where producers in the advanced sector A and consumers achieve significant benefits, whereas the backward sector B realizes a substantial reduction of profits.

Proposition 5: The reallocation of labor from sector B into sector A is a crucial element in the design of a mechanism supporting the first phase of gradual integration.

The second element of improving the mechanism design is to reduce political opposition, which is done indirectly by worsening the best available alternative to continued gradual integration. Suppose that a government policy leads to a decline in producers' profits. Does that imply that producers oppose that policy? Not necessarily: producers would oppose that policy if the alternative were unchanged profits, but if the best available alternative were to produce an even worse outcome, they reluctantly may support that policy.

In our example in table 1, the alternative to trade integration is defined as isolation, which implies a 10% reduction in employment. That alternative is chosen in order to illustrate a mechanism which enforces gradual trade integration: In the first step, interest groups can choose to integrate regionally (from 20 to 4 countries, row <2>) or to remain an isolated outsider (20 countries and isolation, row <6>). As table 1 reveals, the former alternative dominates the latter, since all three interest groups achieve a better outcome in the former case of gradual trade integration, even not considering the effects of labor reallocation. The same reasoning holds for the second step, where interest groups choose between integrating into a world of free trade (from 4 to 1 country, row <4>) or to remain isolated as a region (row <7>) or to remain isolated as individual (row <8>). Again, the choice of trade integration produces better outcomes for all three interest groups than any other alternative.

That idea of worsening the best alternative to a negotiated agreement has become an important concept in negotiation theory. In economic terms, it is also quite intuitive: Suppose that the three Scandinavian countries Norway, Sweden, and Finland apply to join the European Union and further assume that two countries, say Sweden and Finland, have approved the entry in national referenda.

Table 1: Profit and Welfare Changes of Trade Integration

	Δ Profits Sector A	Δ Profits Sector B	Δ Utility Consum.
<1> C=20 to C=1 at structure (i)	- 0.99	- 2.02	+ 0.13
<2> C=20 to C=4 at structure (i)	- 0.41	- 0.84	+ 0.02
<3> C=4 structural change to (ii)	+ 4.48	- 0.49	0
<4> C=4 to C=1 at structure (ii)	- 1.11	- 1.34	+ 0.09
<5> C=1 structural change to (iii)	+ 9.22	- 6.73	0
<6> C=20 to C=20 (conflict) (iii)	- 0.75	- 1.53	- 0.02
<7> C=4 to C=4 (conflict) at (ii)	- 1.16	- 1.40	- 0.03
<8> C=4 to C=20 (conflict') (ii)	- 1.66	- 2.01	- 0.08

Data: adapted from trading block model of my previous paper

Notes: all changes are given as percentages.

model parameters: $\Theta=0.75$, $\alpha=1$, $\beta=1$, $t=0.25$, $ti=0.05$, $g=0.10$, $L=1$.

(i): $\delta=0.25$, $s=0.40$ (ii): $\delta=0.40$, $s=0.25$ (iii): $\delta=0.75$, $s=0.13$

(conflict): $L=0.90$ (conflict'): $L=0.80$

Norway now has the choice to join or to become an isolated outsider, an alternative which is substantially worse than the status quo situation, where all three countries are part of the free-trade area EFTA. Once put into that bad alternative, trade between Norway and its two neighbors would most likely decline substantially, since they substitute some of their previous trade with Norway now with the countries of the European Union. Economists call that phenomenon trade diversion, and usually it is welfare reducing. Coincidentally, it may be exactly that reasoning which led the Norwegian government to schedule its national referendum after those in the two neighboring countries.

Proposition 6: The worsening of the best alternative to integration through an expected increase in trade diversion is a crucial element in the design of a mechanism supporting the second phase of gradual trade integration.

Three Answers and an Application

We can now summarize the answers which evolved for the three initial questions: First, interests of consumers and producers regarding trade integration are generally opposed. Consumers gain through access to a larger variety of products whereas producers in all sectors loose through increased competition. That answer confirms the finding of Grossman and Helpman (1993), who argued that trade integration is most likely politically viable exactly when it is socially harmful. However, that constellation changes once the effects of trade integration *and* labor reallocation are combined and we assume that some myopia exists: consumers and producers in sector A benefit, whereas producers in sector B loose, which implies that net support for integration has increased.

A mechanism combining both trade integration and labor reallocation into the advanced sector would improve the political sustainability. Moreover, a worsening of the best available alternative to integration would also improve the political sustainability. Policymakers would hence intend to design a mechanism which divides trade integration into several phases, where in each phase the political support grows through labor reallocation and where in each phase the political opposition declines through a worsening of alternatives, such as isolation.

Finally, we found that rapid trade integration often is ex-ante rejected whereas it has the potential to be ex-post politically sustainable. Trade integration needs to be more gradual if either (a) domestic opposition from the special interests groups guided by non-economic objectives is substantial (high initial resistance), or (b) initial protection is very high which implies substantial producer losses, or (c) initial comparative advantage is low which implies that consumers' benefits are initially small or even negative.

In the context of Central European countries, these insights might have some relevance: The Czech Republic, Hungary, Poland, and Slovakia concluded a free-trade area agreement in 1992 and started integrating as a region, while they individually also concluded Association Agreements with the European Union envisaging a second phase of integration. The strategy of gradual trade integration might be favored for two reasons: First, it is believed that these countries had developed comparative advantage guided by the former Comecon which is not necessarily compatible with structures of the European Union, it may have even been developed in the "wrong sector". Moreover, there was some pressure from the supply side to delay rapid integration, since members of the European Union felt not prepared for a rapid enlargement.

In that framework, Central European regional integration currently is progressing, external tariffs have been reduced substantially, a more competitive export-sector has evolved, and the only realistic objective is integration into the

European Union, since all other available alternatives would imply isolation. Moreover, foreign capital inflows have supported the process of structural adjustment, which in turn is expected to further boost political support for trade integration. Hence, there seem to be significant parallels to our political economy model of trade integration, and they will be studied in detail in the following two sections.

A Brief Critique

However, there are also some shortcomings of our model: Most importantly, the model assumes that labor is the only factor of production and that labor reallocation occurs without any adjustment costs. In reality, these adjustment costs are very substantial, and often require significant capital. Moreover, we assume that all firms are owned domestically and hence all interests are expressed in the domestic political process. In reality, multinational firms represent an important part of national economies, and their interests need to be modelled individually. They are expected to gain from trade integration and they may provide additional foreign capital which is often crucial to support domestic structural reforms. Hence, it is conceivable that multinational firms are one of the key interest groups supporting trade integration.

Finally, our model reveals very strong symmetry across countries, which is not always realistic, but helps to keep our model tractable. In the context of Central Europe, we have the possibilities of modelling either the entire world

(100 countries), the European continent (20 countries) or only the region (4 countries), and given the symmetry constraints, the second solution is chosen. Not all symmetry constraints are unrealistic, however. Tariffs are often reduced symmetrically, prices also appear to be strongly correlated and are often reduced by very little if the extent of integration is limited. Hence, our model seems to provide a viable framework, which in any particular case needs to be adjusted and interpreted with caution.

4. THE CENTRAL EUROPEAN DEMAND FOR INTEGRATION

"Return to Europe" evolved as a leading vision across Central Europe, and building that bridge between East and West has been a formidable task especially after the revolutions in 1989. The speed of integration has been a central issue in that process, with advocates for gradual regional integration and others for rapid integration into the European Union. Czechoslovakia, Hungary, and Poland signed *Association Agreements* with the EC in December 1991 which envisage economic and political cooperation, an asymmetrical liberalization of trade, technical assistance, and legal reforms. Moreover, these three countries signed the *Central European Free Trade Agreement (CEFTA)* in December 1992 which intends to create a free trade zone by the year 2001. The return to Europe seems to be realized gradually and the political economy of that process of trade integration is summarized in this section.

The trading block model seems to illustrate that gradual integration quite well, but some of its *assumptions* are questionable: First, while western economic agents are assumed to act fully rational, policymakers in Central and Eastern Europe often restrict individual rationality by including an element of ideology. Malkov (1992) calls that cultural phenomenon "disguised rationality". Most of the present policymakers were part of the former opposition, who very much opposed trade integration within Comecon, and who respected different social values. Second, while western governments usually have a wide variety of policy options available, their eastern counterparts are often very restricted by foreign policy agreements and conditionality. Third, productive resources are not fully owned by citizens, since significant foreign investment has flown to Central Europe and since privatization has not yet dismantled all state ownership.

Implications for Political Economy Model

These changes in assumptions have several implications for our political economy model: First, the ideological element of rationality suggests that the fourth domestic political interest group (D) which is guided by non-economic motives is quite important. Moreover, the background of the present policymakers suggests that, at least initially, consumer interests in the governments' objective function have been very important (high parameter y in equation 1). Second, the foreign policy restrictions, the presence of foreign ownership, and the initial presence of state ownership appear to have reduced the initial opposition to trade integration. Third, the nature of the trade agreements contributed to the formation of four main interests: consumers demand full trade liberalization, competitive producers demand more market access to EU markets, restructuring industries demand additional EU technical and financial support, and the government at large demands more cooperation in political and security areas.

Definition of Sectors

These modifications in our model in turn have several implications for the process of selecting a policy of trade integration: At the outset, the definition of sectors becomes more complicated: while some sectors appear to be already competitive, structural reforms in most sectors have still a long way to go. It seems that the so-called sensitive sectors (including agriculture, iron and steel, chemicals, textiles and clothing) are of particular importance. As indicated in table 2, these four sectors accounted in 1989 for more than 40% of output and employment in Central Europe, and an even higher share of their exports. Apparently, most of these sensitive industries have the potential to remain competitive and hence remain part of the advanced sector A in our model.

However, there are some country specific differences: Iron and steel is about twice as important in Czechoslovakia than in its neighboring economies, footwear and textiles are particularly important in Poland, and employment in agriculture is highest in Hungary. As Hughes and Hare (1992) have shown, that picture approximately also reveals the relative competitiveness in Eastern Europe:

Table 2: Output and Employment in Four Sensitive Sectors in Eastern Europe

	Output-Share (%)			Employment (%)			Exports to EC (%)		
	CZ	HU	PL	CZ	HU	PL	CZ	HU	PL
Iron and Steel (ISIC 371)	10.1	7.4	5.5	6.4	4.5	4.3	12.5	4.9	5.3
Chemicals (ISIC 351, 352)	7.1	10.9	7.0	4.6	5.8	5.3	11.6	10.0	6.7
Footwear/ Textiles (ISIC 321-22, 324)	8.3	8.5	12.6	15.7	16.2	19.2	12.6	17.6	11.7
Food Products (ISIC 311, 3312)	18.7	18.0	15.3	6.8	14.8	11.3	8.0	25.3	19.9
Sensitive products	**44.2**	**44.8**	**40.4**	**33.5**	**41.3**	**40.1**	**44.7**	**57.8**	**43.6**

Data: United Nations, Industrial Statistics Yearbook and International Trade Statistics Yearbook, 1989.

Source: Rollo and Smith (1993, page 148).

The former Czechoslovakia has been traditionally strong in engineering and heavy industry, and less developed in the food processing sector. Hungary stands out in light industry and precision engineering, while Poland shows a relatively strong performance in textiles and food processing. Although the data for this analysis are from 1989, the results reveal today's general situation well, except for some sectors where structural reforms have already been successful.

Degree of Liberalization

Whereas most of these sensitive industries appear to be competitive in the European markets, they may not necessarily be competitive in world markets, especially compared with their competitors in South-East Asia.[10/] Wang and Winters (1993) illustrated the effects of trade liberalization in clothing products. They suggested that rapid full liberalization of trade in clothing products in the EU would significantly reduce EU production, would decrease Central European exports to the EU by 21% from its already depressed level, and would dramatically increase imports from East-Asian producers. Obviously, both the EU and Central Europe have therefore chosen a very gradual path to trade liberalization in clothing products.

The same conclusion must be drawn from a recent OECD (1993) study, which projects the effects of gradual (30%) and rapid (100%) trade liberalization for various regions. While nearly all regions benefit substantially more from rapid liberalization, Eastern Europe is the only exception, where GDP levels by the year 2002 would be reduced and are projected to decline by an additional 0.5% in the case of rapid liberalization (OECD, 1993, p.25, table 2). However, these estimates are based on a static model and neglect dynamic effects which might occur from capital inflows, higher savings, or higher productivity. Hence the outcome might be even worse if structural reforms are avoided, and they might be much better if structural reforms are more successful than expected.

10/ The high protection of the European Union in these sectors and their restrictions of Central European imports at least suggests that these sensitive industries in Central Europe are potentially viable in an integrated European market.

Both studies suggest that it is in the best interest from a social welfare perspective for both the European Union and the Central European nations to liberalize gradually and to reinforce structural reforms. Previous enlargements of the EU have illustrated that the cost of structural reforms are often underestimated (Fratzscher, 1994) and that structural reforms and adjustments of macroeconomic policies are more beneficial if completed prior to integration. Both arguments suggest that financial assistance for structural reforms in Central Europe should be significantly increased and that full membership is still a far distance ahead.

Conflicts of Interest

As in our political economy model, the two issues of liberalization and restructuring are at the center of the present conflict of interest in Central Europe: While consumers and the few already competitive producers advocate rapid membership in the European Union and full access to their markets, the majority of producers advocate a substantial increase in funding for structural reforms and a delay of further trade integration. Multinational firms may in principle support further liberalization, but in the case that they are owned by producers in the EU, their domestic European interests may be dominant. Based on our political economy model, the currently observed urgency of Central European governments to join the European Union cannot be explained, unless foreign policy and security aspects obtain absolute priority.

Haaland (1993) illustrated conflicts of interest among producers for the scenario that EFTA countries integrate with the European Union. He projected substantial consumer benefits from that integration, especially if not only trade costs are reduced, but a full market integration occurs. However, he illustrated that while producers in the skill-intensive and service-sectors are expected to gain, similar losses are expected in the capital-intensive sectors. His results show that integration implies a substantial reallocation of productive resources.

Mechanism Design

While comparisons between the integration of EFTA countries into the European Union and the envisaged integration of Central Europe are always troublesome, the basic mechanism in the political economy model appears to be very similar, only the labeling of the gaining and loosing sectors is, of course, different. In both regions, the initial conditions are much in favor of integration: a regional trading area has already been established, tariff protection has declined substantially, and comparative advantage appears to be significant. These initial conditions would suggest that there are export sectors in both regions which would benefit from integration, that the losses of import-competition sectors are limited given the already reduced protection, and that the gains of consumers are positive given the presence of significant comparative advantage and low tariffs.

However, there may be one key difference between EFTA countries and Central Europe: the extent of necessary factor reallocation is much larger in

Central Europe, while the availability of capital to pay for these adjustment costs in much higher in EFTA countries. In both cases, the reallocation of labor into the more productive export sector is a crucial element of a mechanism which enables trade integration to become politically sustainable. We should add that this mechanism must not only enable the shifting of labor across sectors, but also provide the necessary capital for this transformation. In the case of Central Europe, that argument would underline the role of foreign capital as a catalyst for the transformation.

A second important element of a politically sustainable mechanism is the manipulation of available alternatives to integration. Again, the situation in EFTA countries and in Central Europe is similar. Both groups consist of four countries, and each group has significant internal economic relations. If now three members of a group integrate into the European Union and the fourth member lacks the domestic political support, the choice is between two bad options: integrate without the desired domestic political support, or face isolation with likely much higher costs for social welfare (such as higher unemployment and higher protection). That second element of a politically sustainable mechanism hence suggests that groups of countries with significant economic inter-relations should integrate as a block into a larger trading block. That argument would suggest that the three Scandinavian EFTA countries as well as the four Central European countries represent from a political economy perspective an optimal group for trade integration.

5. THE EUROPEAN UNION'S SUPPLY OF INTEGRATION

It appears that the European door is not as open as it is often assumed, and that the interests of the supply side are very dominant in the negotiation of new memberships. The European Union has set some basic criteria applicants must meet (eg. democratic structures), it has also agreed on some basic economic convergence objectives (eg. Maastricht criteria) which are important for applicants, and it has decided to take a very gradual approach to enlargement. That has been consistent with the Northern enlargement in 1973 (United Kingdom, Ireland, and Denmark), the Southern enlargement in 1981/86 (Greece, Spain, and Portugal), and the envisaged EFTA enlargement planned for 1995 (Austria, Norway, Sweden, and Finland).

While our trading block model gives some basic conceptual insights into trade and welfare effects of a world where trading blocks are growing, some modifications in its *assumptions* and in the interpretation of its results are necessary. First, the symmetry assumption must be relaxed since the size of the member countries is quite different. Second, the assumption of liberalized internal trade does not hold in certain sectors, as for instance in agriculture, where substantial deviations from free trade are remaining. Third, the ownership structure of firms has become more complex, there are some firms owned nationally, others are European enterprises, and also multinational companies have expanded.

Implications for the Political Economy Model

The decision making process in the European Union is more complex than in an individual country, so that the modelling of our four interest groups in the political economy model needs to be reconsidered. The European Commission (although not yet directly elected) supposedly represents the European government which optimizes its policy choice given the monetary and electoral contributions by consumers and producers. However, national governments have an important influence on European decisions, which include especially their budgetary contributions and policies on security and migration. These national governments can be modelled as the fourth domestic special interest group in our model.

The role of this special interest group needs to be redefined: In certain issues, the resistance of this interest group is large enough to block policy decisions (huge U_D). This veto power of national governments especially exists if policy decisions imply a regionally unbalanced outcome or require additional financing, such as any enlargement of the EU certainly would. We therefore assume that this special interest group aims to achieve a regional balance.

Besides that particular importance of national governments, the objective function of the European government is often called "producer biased". Indeed, the implementation of the Single European market gives a good example. It was realized to a large degree because of financial support from producers, while consumers had little influence on the outcome, since they not even directly elect the European government. Hence in terms of our model, campaign contributions appear to be more important than electoral votes (low parameter y in equation 1).

Definition of Sectors

When the European Commission negotiated the Association Agreements with several Central European nations, it distinguished two sectors in the liberalization schedule: while the regular sector, supposedly competitive exporters, was asked to liberalize rapidly, the so called sensitive sector, supposedly restructuring import-competing industries, was given extra protection. Hence it seems reasonable to differentiate between these two sectors. While the integration of Central European countries would have a positive effect on the regular sector, there might be substantial costs in the sensitive sector, which includes agriculture, iron and steel, chemicals, textiles and clothing.

Rollo and Smith (1993) produced some estimates about the potential gains and losses which would result from integrating the four Central European countries into the European Union. Although their estimates are based on 1989 data and were criticized for methodological shortcomings, their results are at this point the best available, which at least help to clarify the big picture. As shown in table 3, integration would result in a substantial loss for producers in sensitive sectors, a gain for consumers due to lower prices, and probably lower tariff revenues. While the largest losses for producers are occurring in agriculture, the consumer surplus is most significant in the chemical industry and in agriculture.

Table 3: Size of Gains and Losses for the EU in Four Sensitive Sectors

	Production Change in all EC (%)	Producer Losses (ECU mill)	Consumer Surplus (ECU mill)	Tariff** Revenues(ECU mill)	Δ Net Welfare (Ecu mill)
Iron and Steel	-4.3%	-348.3	+350.1	-417.5	-415.7
Chemicals	-2.9%	-734.8	+1,053.1	-1,183.1	-864.8
Textiles/Clothing	-6.4%	-184.1	+278.1	-334.0	-240.0
Agricult.Products	-6 to -8%*	-3,741.0	+3,972.0	-2,081.0	-1,850.0

*: indicated medium estimates, ranging from -1% for cereals to -10% for oils.

**: assuming no change in EC prices

Source: Rollo and Smith (1993), tables 11 to 16, pp. 154-165.

As indicated in table 3, the total welfare loss for the European Union would be around ECU 3 billion. Agricultural products would account for nearly two-thirds of those losses. In the estimation of tariff losses, the very unlikely assumption has been made that EU prices remain fixed, so that these estimates are likely to be at the upper bounds. However, producer losses of about ECU 5 billion and a 5% decline in production of sensitive sectors should be put into perspective: The European Union spends more than ECU 21 billion each year in structural funds, and the ongoing reform in agriculture reduced employment by 3.8% each year during the 1970s and by 3.3% each year during the 1980s. Hence it appears that the shock in the EU from integrating Central European countries would be relatively modest, even in agriculture.

Conflict of Interests

Besides the two traditional conflicts of interest among consumers and producers and within producers, we must now add a third regional dimension. The most interesting question is how these losses are distributed across European nations. Rollo and Smith (1993) found that the losses are very much concentrated in Greece and Ireland, and to some extend in regions of Italy, Portugal, and Spain, while some gains (abstracting from tariff losses) are expected for the United Kingdom, Germany, France, and Benelux countries. The total producer losses in the member countries (Rollo and Smith, 1993, table 16) range from 0.09% (UK, Germany) to 0.55% of GDP (Greece, Ireland), which again should be compared to more than 3% of GDP for instance Greece each year receives in structural funds.

A more serious conflict of interest comes up when the financing of new membership is discussed. Baldwin (1992) estimated that at least ECU 11 billion would be needed for structural funds in new member-countries, and more recently Baldwin (1994) argued that the total bill of Eastern enlargement including farm and regional subsidies would total more than ECU 58 billion each year, which would require at least a doubling of the European budget. Much of that additional expenditure would come from higher taxes, so that consumers will probably carry the main portion of the enlargement bill, although the governments again are most concerned about the relatively minor losses projected for producers in the sensitive sectors.

Mechanism Design

In the context of the evolution of the European Union, it appears that only a gradual enlargement has been politically sustainable. While political objectives were guiding the initial formation of the European Community, more economic motives dominate today's discussion on an Eastern enlargement. Since every member country has a veto-right on enlargement questions, the regional distribution of gains and losses must be balanced and the power of national governments cannot be underestimated. While adjustment can take place at two different speeds, enlargement can only occur at the smallest common denominator, which makes it a more lengthy and complicated process.

The relatively high importance of producers' interests in the European Union points to further delay of the Eastern enlargement: Rapid integration of Central European countries would imply about ECU 5 billion in producer losses, heavily concentrated in certain sectors and regions, but on the other hand, a delayed enlargement even if it requires additional funds for technical assistance (which were about ECU 1 billion in PHARE funds in 1992 for Central Europe) would be covered by the general budget and be more likely to gain political support.

However, a mechanism may evolve which makes the Eastern enlargement politically more sustainable: European producers may expand their joint-ventures in Central Europe, so that their potential profits from integration more than offset the potential losses in EU markets. Hence the interests of European multinational firms may evolve as a catalyst for further integration. Moreover, urgent political and security concerns may accelerate that tendency. On the other hand, that process is endangered by the growing influence of special interest groups, voiced in particular by some member governments of Southern Europe, who expect to loose most from further integration. Probably a review of national contributions to the European budget and a new allocation of structural funds would provide the most appropriate occasion for creating a mechanism where special interests are balanced and the Eastern enlargement becomes politically more sustainable.

6. CONCLUSIONS

The purpose of this paper was to study the political economy of trade integration both from a theoretically and from a practical view regarding Central European integration. The theoretical section linked a political economy model with a trading block model in order to study the political sustainability of gradual and rapid trade integration. That part identified four main domestic political interest groups which lobby the government with financial contributions or electoral votes to adopt their proposed policy. The optimizing, rational government then chooses the policy of trade integration if initial resistance and expected producer losses are offset by expected producer benefits in the export sector and an expected consumer surplus.

The trading block model extended that framework by studying the effects of sequential trade integration. Six propositions were elaborated, which led to three main results: First, trade integration often implies a conflict of interest both between the two production sectors and also between producers and consumers. Second, rapid trade integration is often ex-ante not politically sustainable, even if it may be ex-post. Third, a mechanism to improve the political sustainability of trade integration can be designed by linking trade integration with factor reallocation and by worsening the best available alternative to integration.

These theoretical insights were then used to study the supply and demand of European integration with respect to Central Europe. On the demand side, it was found that initial conditions are favorable and that regional arrangements such as EFTA and CEFTA promote integration since they imply some factor reallocation and they create isolation as the inferior alternative to continued integration. Moreover, the important role of foreign capital was pointed out since it is essential to finance part of the factor reallocation. These structural reforms need to be implemented to a large extend prior to European integration.

The interests of the European Union in supplying new memberships appear to be dominant and point towards a gradual path where two main obstacles remain: First, producers' interests are dominant in the formation of European policy, although producer losses are estimated much smaller than the overall budgetary cost of integrating Central Europe. However, if European multinationals have an important stake in Central Europe, integration may become more politically sustainable. Second, special interest groups, in particular some national governments, use their veto-rights to enforce a regional balance and may only support further enlargement if budget contributions and structural funds are renegotiated. Although many results are rather suggestive than conclusive, the modelling may provide a viable basis for future research, which could extend the political economy model to include interests of multinational firms, and which could refine the trading block model to include asymmetrical structures.

7. REFERENCES

Baldwin, Richard. (1985). *"The Political Economy of US Import Policy"*. MIT Press: Cambridge, Massachusetts.

Baldwin, Richard. (1989). "The Growth Effects of 1992". *Economic Policy*. 9: 247-281.

Baldwin, Richard. (1992). "An Eastern Enlargement of EFTA". mimeo. Graduate Institute of International Studies. Geneva.

Baldwin, Richard. (1993) "A Domino Theory of Regionalism". NBER Working Paper No. 4465. Cambridge, Massachusetts.

Baldwin, Richard. (1994). *"Towards an Integrated Europe"*. Center for Economic Policy Research: London.

Bernheim, B. Douglas and Michael D. Whinston (1986a). "Common Agency". *Econometrica.* 54: 923-942.

Bernheim, B. Douglas and Michael D. Whinston (1986b). "Menu Auctions, Resource Allocation and Economic Influence". *Quarterly Journal of Economics.* 101: 1-31.

Bernheim, B. Douglas, Peleg Bazalel, and Michael D. Whinston (1987). "Coalition-Proof Nash Equilibria I: Concepts". *Journal of Economic Theory.* 42: 1-12.

Bhagwati, Jagdish (1992). *"Regionalism and Multilateralism"*. CEPR and The World Bank.

Bond, Eric W. and Constantinos Syropoulos. (1993). "Optimality and Stability of Regional Trading Blocks". mimeo. Pennsylvania State University.

Center for Economic Policy Research (CEPR). (1992). *"Is Bigger Better? The Economics of EC Enlargement"*. CEPR: London.

De la Torre, Augusto, and Margaret R. Kelly. (1992). *"Regional Trade Arrangements"*. Occasional Paper No. 92. International Monetary Fund. Washington DC.

De Melo, Jaime and Arvind Panagariya. (1993). *"New Dimensions in Regional Integration"*. CEPR and University of Cambridge: Cambridge (UK).

Deardorff, Alan V. and Robert M. Stern. (1992). "Multilateral Trade Negotiations and Preferential Trading Arrangements". Discussion Paper No. 307. University of Michigan.

Dewatripont, Mathias, and Gérard Roland. (1993). "The Design of Reform Packages Under Uncertainty". CEPR Discussion Paper No. 860. London.

Dixit, L. and J. Stiglitz. (1977). "Monopolistic Competition and Optimum Product Diversity". *American Economic Review*. 67: 297-308.

Edwards, Sebastian. (1990). "The Sequencing of Economic Reform: Analytical Issues and Lessons from Latin American Experience". *The World Economy*. 13: 1-14.

Ethier, Wilfred J. (1988). *"Modern International Economics"*. 2nd edition. Norton & Company: New York.

Fernandez, Raquel, and Dani Rodrik. (1991). "Resistance to Reform: Status Quo and Bias in the Presence of Individual-Specific Uncertainty". *American Economic Review*. 85(5).

Flemming, John and J.M.C. Rollo. (1992). *"Trade, Payments, and Adjustment in Central and Eastern Europe"*. Royal Institute of International Affairs: London.

Fratzscher, Oliver. (1994). "European Integration: Lessons from the South and Prospects for the East". in Schipke and Taylor (eds.): *"The Economics of Transformation: Theory and Practice in the New Market Economies"*. Springer: New York. 191-232.

Grossman, Gene and Elhanan Helpman. (1993). "The Politics of Free Trade Agreements". NBER Working Paper No. 4597. Cambridge, Massachusetts.

Grossman, Gene and Elhanan Helpman. (1994). "Protection for Sale". *American Economic Review*. forthcoming.

Haaland, Jan I. (1993). "Welfare effects of 1992: a General Equilibrium Assessment for EC and EFTA Countries. mimeo. Norwegian School of Economics and Business Administration.

Hamilton, Carl B. and Alan L. Winters. (1992). "Trade with Eastern Europe". *Economic Policy*. 12: 77-116.

Helpman, Elhanan and Paul R. Krugman. (1985). *"Market Structure and Foreign Trade"*. MIT Press: Cambridge, Massachusetts.

Hillman, Ariel. (1989). *"The Political Economy of Protection"*. Harwood Academic Publishers: New York.

Hirschman, Albert O. (1981). *"Essays in Trespassing: Economics to Politics and Beyond"*. Cambridge University Press: Cambridge.

Hughes, Gordon and Paul Hare. (1992). "Industrial Policy and Restructuring in Eastern Europe". *Oxford Review of Economic Policy*. 8(1): 82-104.

Krugman, Paul R. (1980). "Scale Economies, Product Differentiation, and the Pattern of Trade". *American Economic Review*. 70: 950-959.

Krugman, Paul R. (1991a). "Is Bilateralism bad?". in E. Helpman and A. Razin (eds.) *"International Trade and Trade Policy"*. MIT Press: Cambridge, Massachusetts.

Krugman, Paul R. (1991b). "The Move toward Free Trade Zones". *Economic Review* (Kansas). November 1991: 5-25.

Krugman, Paul R. (1993). *"Regionalism versus Multilateralism: analytical notes"*. in: Jaime De Melo and Arvind Panagariya (eds): "New Dimensions in regional integration". CEPR and University of Cambridge: Cambridge.

Lawrence, Robert Z. (1991). "Emerging Regional Arrangements: Building Blocks or Stumbling Blocks?". in: *"Finance and the International Economy"*. Amex Bank Review. Oxford University Press: Oxford.

Lawrence, Robert Z. (1994). "Regionalism, Multilateralism, and Deeper Integration". mimeo. Harvard University: Cambridge, Massachusetts.

Leamer, Edward E. (1984). *"Sources of International Comparative Advantage: Theory and Evidence"*. MIT Press: Cambridge, Massachusetts.

Leamer, Edward E. (1992). "Testing Trade Theory". NBER Working Paper No. 3958. Cambridge, Massachusetts.

Malkov, Leonid P. (1992). "How Rational is the Behavior of Economic Agents in Russia?". *Comparative Economic Studies*. 34(1): 26-40.

Mayer, Wolfgang. (1984). "Endogenous Tariff Formation". *American Economic Review*. 74: 970-985.

McKinnon, Ronald L. (1991). *"The Order of Economic Liberalization: Financial Control in the Transition to a Market Economy"*. Johns Hopkins University Press: Baltimore.

Michalski, Anna and Helen Wallace. (1992). *"The European Community: the Challenge of Enlargement"*. Royal Institute of International Affairs: London.

Midford, Paul. (1993). "International Trade and Domestic Politics: Improving Rogowski's model of Political Alignments". *International Organization.* 4: 535-564.

OECD Development Center. (1993). "Trade Liberalization: what's at stake ?". by Ian Goldin and D. van der Mensbrugghe. OECD Policy Brief No. 5.

Olson, Mancur. (1965). *"The Logic of Collective Action"*. Harvard University Press: Cambridge, Massachusetts.

Perroni, Carlo and John Whalley. (1994). "The New Regionalism: Trade Liberalization or Insurance?". NBER Working Paper No. 4626. January 1994. Cambridge, Massachusetts.

Richardson, Martin. (1992). "Some Implications of Internal Trade in a Free Trade Area". Working Paper No. 92-01. Department of Economics. Georgetown University.

Rodrik, Dani. (1990). "How should Structural Adjustment Programs be designed?". *World Development.* 18(7): 933-947.

Rodrik, Dani. (1992). "The Positive Economics of Policy Reform". mimeo. Columbia University.

Rogowski, Ronald. (1989). *"Commerce and Coalitions: How Trade Affects Domestic Political Alignments"*. Princeton University Press: Princeton.

Rollo, Jim and Alasdair Smith. (1993). "EC Trade with Eastern Europe". *Economic Policy*. April 1993. 13: 139-181.

Schelling, Thomas C. (1960). *"The Strategy of Conflict"*. Harvard University Press: Cambridge, Massachusetts.

Staiger, Robert W. (1994). "A Theory of Gradual Trade Liberalization". NBER Working Paper No. 4620. January 1994. Cambridge, Massachusetts.

Stolper, Wolfgang F. and Paul A. Samuelson. (1941). "Protection and Real Wages". *Review of Economic Studies*. 9: 71.

Viner, Jacob. (1950). *"The Customs Union Issue"*. Carnegie Endowment for International Peace: New York.

Wang, Zhen Kun and L. Alan Winters. (1993). "Liberalizing EC Imports of Clothing from Eastern Europe". Discussion Paper 93-05. University of Birmingham.

Wei, Shang-Jin (1993). "Gradualism and Big Bang: Speed and Sustainability of Reforms". mimeo. Harvard University: Cambridge, Massachusetts.

Winters, L. Alan and Anthony Venables. (1991). *"European Integration: trade and industry"*. Cambridge University Press: Cambridge.

8. APPENDIX-I: OBJECTIVE FUNCTIONS FOR CONSUMERS AND PRODUCERS

Equations (4) and (5) in the main text presented the objective functions for consumers and producers. This appendix derives these objective functions from the trading block model which was in detail elaborated in my previous paper. In Part <A>, we recall the social welfare function and the consumption function from the previous paper, which produce the objective function of the consumer. Part <B> is an intermediate step where the demand function is derived. It is then used in part <C> in order to derive the operating profit function which is the objective function of the producers in our political economy model. The equations referred to have been derived in detail in the appendix of the open-economy-model in chapter I.

<A> Social Welfare Function of the Consumer:

From equation (A-19) we recall the social welfare function:

$$U = [\delta + (1-\delta) * (\frac{\beta - s}{\beta})^{\theta * \theta}] * (\frac{1-\theta}{\alpha}) * L * K * [1 + I + H] \ * \ (c_{i_{AA}})^{\theta} \qquad \text{(B-1)}$$

with the following definitions for parameters I, H, and K:

$$I := (\frac{N}{C} - 1) * (1 + ti)^{\frac{1}{\theta - 1}}$$

$$H := (N - \frac{N}{C}) * (\frac{1}{1-g}) * (\frac{1}{1-g} + t)^{\frac{1}{\theta - 1}} \qquad \text{(B-2)}$$

$$K := \delta + (1-\delta) * (\frac{\beta - s}{\beta})^{\theta}$$

and with the following consumption function recalled from equation (A-18):

$$c_{i_{AA}} = (\frac{\alpha}{\beta - s}) * (\frac{\theta}{1-\theta}) * \frac{1}{L} * \frac{1}{K} * \frac{1}{[1 + (1 - K * ti) * I + (1 - K * t) * H]} \qquad \text{(B-3)}$$

which combined leads to the social welfare function presented in equation (4) of the main text.

<B> Demand Function:

From equation (A-3) we can derive the production share in an open economy:

$$x_{i_A} = [\delta * L * c_{i_{AA}} + (1-\delta) * L * c_{i_{BA}}] * [1 + I + H] \tag{B-4}$$

The relationship between the two consumption shares can be recalled from equation (A-17):

$$c_{i_{BA}} = c_{i_{AA}} * \left(\frac{\beta - s}{\beta}\right)^{\theta} \tag{B-5}$$

Combining the three above equations, we derive the demand function:

$$\begin{aligned} x_{i_A} &= [\delta + (1-\delta) * (\frac{\beta - s}{\beta})^{\theta}] * L * c_{i_{AA}} * [1 + I + H] \\ \leftrightarrow \quad x_{i_A} &= (\frac{\alpha}{\beta - s}) * (\frac{\theta}{1-\theta}) * [\frac{1 + I + H}{1 + (1 - K * ti) * I + (1 - K * t) * H}] \end{aligned} \tag{B-6}$$

<C> Operating Profit Function of the Producers:

Operating profits are defined as (number of products sold) times (price - marginal cost), where the pricing was derived in equation (A-5):

$$\pi_A = n_A * x_{i_A} * [p_A - w_A * (\beta - s)] = n_A * x_{i_A} * w_A * (\beta - s) * (\frac{1-\theta}{\theta}) \tag{B-7}$$

Given the demand function in equation (B-6) we derive the operating profit function of producers in sector A:

$$\pi_A = \delta * L * w_A * (1-\theta) * [\frac{1+I+H}{1+(1-K*ti)*I+(1-K*t)*H}] \tag{B-8}$$

Similarly, the following operating profit function for producers in sector B is derived, which is also presented in equation (5) of the main text:

$$\pi_B = (1-\delta) * L * w_A * (\frac{\beta-s}{\beta})^{\theta} * (1-\theta) * [\frac{1+I+H}{1+(1-K*ti)*I+(1-K*t)*H}] \tag{B-9}$$

FDI: The Neglected Twin of Trade

-- A Substitute or a Complement ?

Abstract:

Chapter III asks whether foreign direct investment (FDI) is a substitute or complement for international trade, since both possibilities are modelled in the theory of multinational firms. A gravity model estimates the cumulative effect for a sample of 63 countries and suggests that FDI inflows *reduce* overall trade and in some cases deteriorate the trade balance. Three channels are identified in case studies of Spain, Mexico, and Thailand but need to be quantified in further research. Predictions should not be based on the gravity model because it appears structurally unstable.

Keywords: foreign direct investment; international trade; multinational firms; empirical modeling; gravity model.

1. INTRODUCTION

Foreign Direct Investment[1/] (FDI) is becoming increasingly important, yet it is widely misunderstood. Characteristics range from "technology vehicle for growth" to "source of deficit financing" and "job-killer from abroad". Recently, attitudes in many countries have shifted much in favor of FDI, and in some cases FDI inflows account for more than 3% of GNP (Spain, Mexico, Thailand). Indeed, growth rates for FDI during the 1980s were more than twice the growth rates of trade and GNP.

The positive effects of foreign direct investment are widely understood, they include easing of the external constraint, lowering the domestic interest rates, increasing productivity, and often higher investment and growth. However, foreign capital inflows and especially FDI can have some drawbacks: increasing foreign ownership, risk of reversal and repatriation of profits, initial appreciation of the real exchange rate, and a deterioration of the trade balance. These drawbacks have long been neglected, and this essay looks at the implications of FDI on trade, first by reviewing the main propositions from microeconomic

---

1/ FDI is defined as "investment that is made to acquire a lasting interest in an enterprise operating in an economy other than that of the investor, the investor's purpose being to have an effective voice in the management of the enterprise" (IMF, 1977, par. 408). Most countries require 10% ownership as minimum of "an effective voice", but that ratio varies widely, for instance it is 20% in France and Britain and 25% in Germany.

theory, then by constructing an empirical model, and finally by illustrating some issues for further research.

Graham and Krugman (1991, page 64) concluded in the context of the United States that the direct effects of FDI on trade are not important. This essay simply questions that assertion without entering a value-loaded discussion on general economic and political costs and benefits of FDI. Our analysis shows for a sample of 63 countries that FDI inflows in general tend to reduce the level of trade and in some cases also deteriorate the trade balance.

In the following part, the historical development of trade and FDI is outlined, showing that both have led to increased economic integration. Empirical data illustrate the dramatic rise of FDI during the 1980s. Then we study how FDI is explained in the theory of multinational firms and address some data issues. With the help of a gravity model of international trade for a sample of 63 countries, we then study the effect of FDI on trade and distinguish between the effects of stocks and flows. However, we also need to be aware of some pitfalls of the gravity model, which should only be used to study *what* happened, but not *why* something happened. We conclude the analysis by identifying a list of issues for further research, which are motivated by insights from three country case studies.

2. FDI AND TRADE AS VEHICLES OF GLOBAL INTEGRATION

Trade Structure and Economic Development

Structural shifts in economic development have produced expanding international trade and more recently expanding flows of foreign direct investment. Back in the 18th century, land and labor were the key elements of comparative advantage, and most international trade consisted of raw materials and agricultural products. At that point, these sectors also employed most of the laborforce. By the 19th century in most of Europe, manufacturing had become the predominant sector and the pattern of comparative advantage changed. Europe exported manufactured goods in exchange for raw materials from developing regions. Already, some sort of foreign investment existed, especially by British companies in former colonies.

By the middle of the 20th century, manufacturing was still the predominant sector in most advanced economies, and trade in manufacturing goods kept growing. However, the pattern of exchange changed again: so far, manufacturing goods from different sectors were exchanged for each other, for instance computers for machinery, in what is called inter-industry trade. More recently, most international trade has been conducted as intra-industry trade, where for instance different brands of cars are traded for each other. Advanced economies today trade more than two thirds of their products within one sector.

During the last decades, a more integrated global economy has evolved. GATT became an important institution which helped to facilitate the growth of trade through multilateral tariff reductions and a most-favored-nation status. Today however, the service sectors have become the fastest growing parts of advanced economies, and again the pattern of comparative advantage has changed. Now many high-tech services such as financial and information services are traded in exchange for manufacturing products. Moreover, firms have become more international and integrated horizontally. US software developers may employ labor in India to take advantage of wage differentials and low-cost communications, Japanese carmakers may build factories in Britain to circumvent import restrictions, and London based brokerage firms may open a New York subsidiary to expand their market share in the US.

As illustrated in the three previous examples, *direct investment* (in Indian labor, in British car factories, or in a New York office) often proves more effective than international trade. Especially the rapid expansion of the service sector with the growing pressure for more globalization led to increased foreign investment. We distinguish two categories of foreign investment according to the investor's interest to acquire ownership: Investment made with the objective to acquire a "lasting interest" (usually more than 10% ownership, cf. footnote 1) is called *foreign direct investment* (FDI), whereas investment in bonds and corporate equities without a management interest is called *portfolio investment*. During the 1980s, a large part of portfolio investment shifted towards direct investment.

FDI and Trade as "Twins"

It appears that foreign trade and FDI are conceptually similar, both have evolved as mechanisms for integrating international markets and both have contributed to gains in efficiency and to higher growth. In the 1950s, trade liberalization stimulated growth through improved efficiency in manufacturing sectors facing import competition, and in the 1980s, FDI led to efficiency gains in service sectors by expanding international competition. Similarly, in the 1950s, the shift to convertible currencies boosted international trade, and in the 1980s, the opening of capital markets acted as a catalyst for growing FDI.

Foreign direct investment has been called the "twin" of international trade (Julius, 1991), but it is a long neglected twin. Indeed, even today global FDI accounts for barely 10% the size of global trade. However, annual growth rates from 1985-90 were 33% for FDI flows, compared to 12% for world GNP, and 13% for world trade in goods and services. Moreover, the stock of FDI today accounts for more than 8% of world GNP. In Germany for example, more than 17% of assets are owned by foreign capital, and foreign firms account for about 18% of total sales (Economist, 1990).

The volume of foreign direct investment rose from $ 50 billion in 1980 to more than $ 190 billion in 1990, as indicated in table 1. Today a share of 13% of FDI inflows is going to developing countries, the main share of it to South-East Asia. The developing countries' share in today's stock of FDI is still less than 4%, up from 1.5% in 1980 (Jungnickel, 1993). Moreover, the sectoral patterns have shifted from manufacturing more into the services sector.

Table 1: Flows of Foreign Investment ($ billion)

Countries	**Outflows**		**Inflows**	
	1980	**1990**	**1980**	**1990**
United States	19.2	33.4	16.9	37.2
Japan	2.4	48.0	0.3	1.7
Germany	4.0	22.3	0.4	1.5
France	3.1	27.1	3.3	9.1
Italy	0.8	7.1	0.6	6.3
United Kingdom	11.3	20.8	10.1	33.7
Canada	2.7	1.2	0.7	5.7
OECD Total	*48.9*	*193.5*	*38.1*	*126.7*
Asian NIEs	0.1	0.4	2.8	13.2
Latin America	..	..	5.4	7.0

Sources: OECD, IMF, and UN Center for Transnational Corporations (1992)

However, the comparison between the size of FDI and international trade is conceptually not correct. FDI itself is only the initial vehicle to access foreign markets, and the additional local purchases from suppliers and sales to customers are more analogous for a comparison with the size of total trade. UNCTC (1992) estimated that more than one quarter of world GNP is accounted for by sales of foreign affiliates, and on top of that, about 25% of world trade is conducted as intra-company transactions. Hence, FDI today may be of equal magnitude and importance as international trade.

Differences in FDI

From a *country perspective*, FDI is a coin with two sides: It is desirable as a vehicle for technology and skills transfer and as a form of capital inflow without any debt-servicing obligation. As Graham and Krugman (1991) pointed out, FDI often increases productivity, enhances structural change, and contributes to economic growth. On the other side, in a worst case scenario, multinational enterprises may acquire local firms with the objective to deter competition and enhance an oligopolistic market structure, expatriate profits, and reduce employment. From a *company perspective*, FDI can serve two main purposes: it can be *factor-based*, providing access to cheap raw materials, labor, and technologies; or it can be *market-based*, facilitating exports or also substituting for them. Academics and business consultants have produced substantial work explaining FDI more in detail, starting with Dunning (1958), Kindleberger (1969) and his student Hymer (1976), and good reviews are provided by Casson (1987) and Julius (1991).

This paper elaborates especially the relationship between FDI and trade. In the literature, four types of FDI are distinguished according to their effect on international trade:[2]

<a> *trade substituting FDI*: import-substituting activities

<b> *trade promoting FDI*: offshore operation for international markets

<c> *trade complementing FDI*: intra-industry support facilities abroad

<d> *trade diverting FDI*: main purpose to circumvent trade barriers.

The second and third categories of FDI are believed to increase international trade, whereas the first and fourth categories supposedly reduce or divert international trade. That gives us a first general idea about the possible impact of FDI on trade, but it is difficult to quantify these four components and to differentiate between effects on imports and exports. Therefore, we will in the following review which intuition the theory of multinational firms suggests, before we estimate a gravity model of world trade.

3. FDI AND THE THEORY OF MULTINATIONAL FIRMS

Conventional Trade Theory

The most fundamental idea in conventional trade theory is *comparative advantage*, which considers differences in economic structure as basis for trade,

2/ This part draws on the analysis of Ariff (1989).

and which is formally modelled in the Heckscher-Ohlin theory. However, that theory does not accommodate multinational firms, since it assumes neoclassical firms as the central agent, and only addresses general effects arising from changes in factor endowments. It assumes that differences in factor endowments generate differences in factor rewards, which in turn generate trade and/or allow factor movements in order to equalize factor prices. If factors are mobile, factor endowments between countries need to become more similar in order to achieve factor price equalization, which according to the Rybczynski theorem implies that trade between these countries declines. Hence, according to conventional trade theory, *international trade and international investment should be negatively correlated.*

New Trade Theory

Two new concepts are introduced by the *new trade theory*: economies of scale and imperfect competition. The fundamental idea in the new trade theory is that countries trade in order to become more specialized, aiming to become more productive by producing fewer goods on a larger scale, so that markets become more competitive. Whereas the conventional theory focused mainly on factor-based motivations of foreign direct investment, the new theory of trade adds some market-based motivations. The existence of multinational firms is built on *locational advantages* (producing abroad instead of exporting), on *ownership advantages* (a patent or managerial ability utilized abroad), and on *internalization advantages* (manufacturing abroad rather than licensing). These three advantages of multinational firms have been studied in detail by Kindleberger (1969), Hymer (1976), Dunning (1977 and 1981), and Rugman (1980). They were translated into new theories of international trade by Krugman (1979), Lancaster (1980), Helpman (1984), and Helpman and Krugman (1985).

We illustrate the insights from new trade theories with three examples: Models of *monopolistic competition* (eg. Krugman 1980 and Lancaster 1980) allow factor mobility and suggest that factor movements are substitutes for international trade, and that they are in general more effective than trade to achieve factor price equalization. More sophisticated models incorporated the *internalization advantage* of multinational firms (Markusen 1984 and Ethier 1986), and more recently Ethier (1992) developed a model for trade in services, which allows two-way flows of FDI, explains FDI flows among very similar countries, and suggests that international trade and FDI may be complementary. Moreover, models incorporating *intermediate products* (Helpman 1984, and Helpman and Krugman 1985) suggest that FDI often changes the product composition of trade and leads to additional trade in other product categories, establishing a complementary relationship between FDI and trade. Hence, *the new trade theory presents a large variety of models which allow both for complementarity and substitution between international trade and foreign direct investment.*

Causality between FDI and Trade

During the last three decades, international trade has expanded first, and FDI has only started to expand during the 1980s. In this sense, increasing trade has caused increasing FDI. The *causes of expanding FDI* have been the subject of a large variety of studies, which list several factors, such as political stability, economic growth, financial incentives, and also expanding trade. This essay, however, focuses of the effects of FDI, and in particular on the *effects of FDI on trade*. Although expanding trade may have initially led to expanding FDI, the question is whether expanding FDI per se leads to expanding or contracting trade.

This question can be approached from two perspectives, one short-term and one medium-term: The theory of multinational firms suggests that expanding FDI may initially lead to expanding trade, and only after several cycles of expanding FDI and trade, there appears a tendency for trade to contract. Consider for instance an IBM greenfield investment in Spain, initially motivated by large exports of computers from the US to Spain. The greenfield investment first requires building a factory, and some building material may be imported from the US, causing trade to increase. Indeed, it is shown empirically that foreign-owned firms (IBM in Spain) have a stronger tendency to initially source abroad (in the US) than do domestic (Spanish) firms (Graham and Krugman, 1991). After construction of the IBM factory, some engineers need to be trained and some education material may be imported from the US, afterwards maybe some marketing and financial services, etc. Initially, overall trade between Spain and the US may increase, if the additional trade in building materials more than offsets the decline in trade of computers. The changing product mix of trade may lead to additional FDI, but after several cycles, IBM sources predominantly in Spain and trade between the US and Spain declines.

Empirically, it is very difficult to determine the exact causality between trade and FDI, and very often we observe bi-directional causality. We should hence not attempt to quantify the short-term effect of one additional dollar of FDI on trade, but only focus on the main question, whether one additional dollar in FDI in the medium-term increases or decreases the level of trade.

Symmetry Constraints

It is necessary to choose between two hypotheses: Does a greenfield investment of IBM in Spain, ceteris paribus, only affect trade between the US and Spain or does it also affect trade between Spain and France, for instance trade in Bull computers? The latter seems more likely, and therefore we assume in our analysis that FDI affects trade on a multilateral basis. Moreover, we also make the simplifying assumption that any one dollar in FDI inflows in Spain has the same impact on Spain's trade with the rest of the world, in other words one dollar of FDI inflows coming either from IBM or from Bull or from Siemens has the same impact on Spanish trade. That of course is a constraint in our analysis, but it allows us to look at the global effects of FDI on trade by aggregating all bilateral FDI inflows into one total, and to avoid serious estimation problems by modeling many close to zero bilateral FDI inflows, as for instance FDI inflows to Spain from Micronesia.

Moreover, we also impose a symmetry constraint by assuming that effects of FDI *outflows* are opposite to those of FDI *inflows*: That means, if FDI inflows substitute trade, then FDI outflows complement trade, which implies that trade shifts between trading partners as for instance illustrated in appendix 1: the country with net FDI outflows (country A) increases its trade by shifting it towards the rest of the world (country C) and the country with FDI inflows (country B) reduces its trade. This model suggests a negative relationship between international trade and FDI, since FDI flows from country A to country B have ceteris paribus substituted for trade.

This model may only be a rough approximation of reality, but we could imagine an example with Japan at the place of country A (FDI outflows), the United States at the place of country B (FDI inflows), and the rest of the world at the place of country C (supposedly no FDI flows). During the 1980s, Japan indeed had large FDI outflows and a large trade surplus both with the US and the rest of the world. At the same time, the US had large FDI inflows and a large trade deficit both with Japan and the rest of the world, and the share of US trade in total world trade declined. The problem with this simplified model is its tendency to over-simplify, for instance world trade is driven by many other factors besides FDI flows (such as exchange rate movements, changes in productivity, etc). At this point, we only study the *cumulative effect* of FDI on trade, and will point out the likely composition of this effect in a later section on macroeconomic considerations.

Gross Versus Net FDI

From a theoretical point of view, there are good reasons to take either gross or net FDI in order to illustrate their cumulative effect on trade. From a practical point of view, net flows of FDI are more readily available and are for instance reported in the International Financial Statistics of the IMF. The differences between gross and net FDI values are significant especially for the US and the UK, which both have large FDI inflows and outflows, but they are negligible for Japan and Germany (nearly all outflows) and for most developing countries (nearly all inflows).

Different measures of FDI are in used for different purposes: On the one hand, gross FDI values are often used if different flows are considered as independent movements without significant reversals (for instance IBM pulling in and out of Spain in the same year), whereas on the other hand, net FDI values are more meaningful for studying the cumulative effects of FDI on trade especially in a model with the above outlined symmetry assumptions. Basically, both gross and net FDI are telling part of the story, and any choice has some drawbacks. We decided to take net FDI values, because they seem more appropriate to study our question of cumulative effects of FDI on trade, because they are appear to be less volatile than gross values, and because they are more readily available in a common classification. However, we should keep in mind that our coefficients therefore underestimate the effects of FDI on trade in some cases, especially for the US and the UK with large ratios of gross to net FDI.

FDI Stocks Versus Flows

We already mentioned the important time dimension of FDI, since FDI inflows may in the short-term lead to increased imports and a change in the product mix of trade, whereas in the medium-term, when the foreign owned companies start sourcing domestically and produce for the domestic market (often substituting for imports), overall trade in the FDI receiving country may decline. Therefore, we distinguish between the effect of *net FDI flows* on trade and the effect of the *FDI stock* on trade. We assume that the FDI stock (as any other capital stock) is depreciating over time, approximately at a rate of 10% per year which is usually assumed in the literature.

However, the assumption that the FDI stock is depreciating is not without problems: in the case of new greenfield investment, capital usually depreciates and retained earnings which are reinvested are counted as new FDI inflows, so that in this case we can assume that the stock of FDI does depreciate. On the other hand, in the case of share holdings, only reinvested dividends are counted as additional FDI inflows, whereas the growth of the market value of shares does not count as additional FDI. In the latter case, the FDI stock might actually grow or only depreciate at the rate of inflation, usually at less than 10% per year. Most FDI data, however, do not distinguish between the two types of greenfield investments and share holdings, so that for the purpose of our analysis we have to treat both types in the same way.

The importance of FDI stocks and flows also changed significantly during the 1980s: FDI flows quadrupled from $ 50 billion in 1980 to more than $ 190 billion in 1990, and the stock of FDI rose from a very low base to more than 8% of world GNP in 1990. FDI flows were hence more significant in the beginning of the 1980s, whereas stocks became more important towards the end of the decade, especially when FDI flows stagnated during 1990. The rate of depreciation we use to calculate FDI stocks is therefore not of primary importance, because most of the stocks have been accumulated in very recent years. We decided to follow the common approach of the literature, and calculated FDI stocks as the sum of net FDI flows starting in 1975 with an annual depreciation of 10%. Moreover, we calculated FDI inflows as the sum of the last two years net FDI flows, so that the volatility to some degree is reduced and that a certain time lag is incorporated which often occurs before FDI flows have an impact on trade (eg. time needed for setup or construction). We always calculate FDI stocks and flows as a ratio over GNP, in order to give equal weights to significant FDI flows in small and medium-sized economies and not only to large absolute flows of Japan, the US, and the UK. However, this approach tends to underestimate the impact of FDI on trade in cases where a country has a large ratio of gross to net FDI flows and where a country has an initially large ratio of FDI stocks to flows.

Resuming, our analysis of the effects of FDI on trade poses a series of difficulties: First, it is difficult to measure FDI flows per se, since they not only include capital movements but also the transfer of non-tangibles (such as patents or ideas) which are hard to value. Moreover, it is difficult to quantify the effect of FDI on trade, because FDI at the same time is a dependent and independent variable, at the same time being caused by previous trade and having effects on future trade. Second, we only study the cumulative effect of FDI on trade, assuming that FDI has implications on the multilateral structure of trade, and that some strong symmetry conditions hold. Third, we distinguish between effects of net FDI flows on trade and effects of depreciating FDI stocks on trade, where in some cases we underestimate the coefficients. Finally, it is our primary objective to analyze the cumulative impact of FDI on trade, whereas we can only briefly illustrate possible channels through which this impact is realized in a section outlining issues for future research.

4. DATA MATERIAL

Some other issues about our data need to be raised. The classification of FDI varies widely across countries, because the definitions of "foreign" and "significant ownership" are problematic. First, a number of firms are reported both as foreign-owned and as a US parent by the US Bureau of Economic Analysis (for instance Du Pont, as reported by Graham and Krugman, 1991, page 10), because their headquarters are located in the US but a significant part of their capital is held abroad. Second, the standard of measuring an "effective voice in management" via a minimum ownership share is not consistent across countries: in Germany, for instance, the minimum share is 25%, in France it is 20%, and in the US it is 10%.

FDI as a measure in the balance of payments includes three components: net change in equities of companies held by foreign investors, retained and reinvested earnings of these shares, and net intra-firm loans from foreign investors to these foreign-owned companies. Especially the last two components are difficult to measure and (for instance for tax reasons) are not always correctly reported by multinational firms. Hence we need to consider the FDI measure with a good grain of caution, although IMF data with a common classification seem to be more reliable than national FDI data.

Even besides these definitional issues, some significant changes in the structure of FDI occurred during the 1980s. As Graham and Krugman (1991, page 24) pointed out, Japan has been the world's principal exporter of portfolio capital, defined as investments in bonds and equities without "effective ownership" interests. However, during the 1980s, the composition of Japanese outward investment shifted largely away from portfolio to foreign direct investment, in part because previous portfolio investment accumulated and reached a share of ownership which became significant according to our definition. Although previously classified as portfolio investment and then reclassified as foreign direct investment, it is not clear that any original interests linked with these investments have changed. We therefore decided to include portfolio investment into our analysis, because a large portion of Japanese portfolio investment during the 1980s may have been very similar to what we defined as foreign direct investment.

We define stocks and flows of portfolio investment (PFI) analogous to our measures of foreign direct investment (FDI), although the depreciation of the PFI stocks becomes even more dubious than before. Because of the volatility of PFI, we would expect PFI stocks to have a more significant effect on trade than PFI flows. We would also expect PFI stocks to be more important in 1980 than in 1985 or 1990, because of the above mentioned shifts in classifications. Moreover, we would expect that net FDI and net PFI flows averaged over two or three years are highly correlated, because supposedly they are caused by common factors, such as economic growth, financial incentives, political stability, etc.

5. A Gravity Model of International Trade and FDI

This section now asks whether the complementary or substitutive relationship between international trade and foreign direct investment is empirically borne out. We use a gravity model of international trade to answer that question, since that model has proven very robust. It has been used extensively in empirical international economics to estimate volume and direction of bilateral trade flows, and Deardorff (1984) indeed suggested that it has shown the best empirical performance in explaining international trade flows. Originally, the model stems from Linnemann (1966), who proposed it as a pragmatic way to combine the three independent variables -- importers' demand, exporters' supply, and the costs of doing business -- in order to determine bilateral international trade flows.

Using the gravity model in its empirical robustness, we also need to be aware that it has not been thoroughly derived from economic theory. Deardorff (1984) noted that it tells us about *what* happens in international trade, but it doesn't necessarily tell us *why* that happens. Several authors attempted to derive a solid theoretical underpinning for the model, most notably Anderson (1979), Bergstrand (1985), and Helpman and Krugman (1985), but none of them exactly derived the model in its simplicity. Bergstrand (1985 and 1989) derived a generalized version of the gravity model from a general equilibrium framework based on non-homothetic utility functions and differentiated products structures.

His final equation described trade flows of a good from i to j as a multiplicative function of country i's income, country j's income, country j's income per capita, trading cost variables, complex price terms, and various endowment and factor intensity variables.

Our gravity model is very close to that structure derived by Bergstrand, except that we omit the complex price terms. We are using a log-linear form in order to express the multiplicative character. First, we abstract from FDI as an independent variable, and only attempt to determine a set of independent variables which determine international trade. Then, we can control for these independent variables and study the impact of an additional independent variable FDI, which we differentiate between stock and flows. Hence our basic model has the form expressed in equation (1), where the last three variables are dummies used to indicate a common border, a common language, or a common trading block between trading partners i and j. All other variables are used in the log form, so that the coefficients indicate elasticities.

$$\begin{aligned} trade_{(i to j)} = \; & const + \alpha_1 * GNP_i + \alpha_2 * GNP_j + \alpha_3 * (GNP/cap)_i + \alpha_4 * (GNP/cap)_j \\ & + \alpha_5 * distance_{ij} + \alpha_6 * adjacency_{ij} + \alpha_7 * language_{ij} + \alpha_8 * block_{ij} \end{aligned} \tag{1}$$

The three most important factors in explaining bilateral trade flows are probably the economic size of countries, their economic openness, and the geographical distance between them. These factors are the essence of the gravity model. The potential supply of exports and demand of imports depends on the overall size of the country, measured by its GNP. Since the GNP for both trading partners enters in a multiplicative form, we would expect that two countries of similar size trade more with each other than two countries of very different sizes. Moreover, countries' openness ratio can be proxied by its population, since several studies have shown that a larger population has a negative effect on economic openness, given that larger countries become more self sufficient. Recently, some authors suggested to use the proxy GNP/capita (eg. Frankel and Wei, 1993), and we would expect that this coefficient is positive. Finally, the main obstacles to trade are transaction costs and the cost of transportation, which both decrease for countries close to each other. These obstacles to trade are proxied by the geographical distance, measured as the distance between its two main trading centers, and we would expect it to show a significant negative coefficient.

We improve the gravity model by adding a few dummy variables expressing special trade relationships between countries which belong to a common trading area, which share a common border, and which share a common language, which are all believed to reduce the transaction costs of trade. We actually introduce three different dummy variables for the European Union, for the Western Hemisphere, and for the South-East Asian area. Most likely, all coefficients of these dummy variables should be positive, but maybe not all of them significant.

We proceed in three steps: First, we calculate the regression specified above for three time periods with data for 1980, 1985, and 1990 and differentiate between imports, exports, and total trade (imports plus exports, all measured in US dollars). We then check the signs of the coefficients and the goodness of fit measured by an adjusted R-squared. Second, we extend the above regression by introducing factor endowments (as suggested in Bergstrand's 1989 model) and check whether trade follows the traditional factor endowments theory. Third, we control for all these independent variables and add foreign direct investment as an independent variable in order to study the impact of FDI on international trade. As indicated in appendix 3d, our data sample includes 63 countries and hence 1953 (=63*62/2) observations.

Basic Model

First, the results of our basic model are shown in appendix 2. They confirm our intuition: a 1% increase in GNP in both countries increases trade by 1.5% (sum of coefficients $\alpha 1$ and $\alpha 2$), suggesting that our experience of trade growing faster than GNP is borne out empirically. Also, countries with larger populations ceteris paribus trade less (positive $\alpha 3$ and $\alpha 4$). Finally, distance between countries appears to be very significant, for each additional 1000 miles in distance, trade between those partners declines by more than one third [exp (-0.50)].

Interesting results are also shown by the dummy variable coefficients: Neighboring countries trade twice [exp(0.70)] of the amount that non-neighbors trade, and if trading partners share a common language (English, Spanish, French, Portuguese, Chinese, Arabic) their trade on average increases by 60% [exp(0.50)]. Countries within the EC today trade an additional 80% with each other, and countries in East Asia an additional 800%. It should however be noted that these coefficients are very unstable and probably capture a lot of left-out variable bias.

Endowment Data

We now add an additional variable for factor endowments to see whether countries trade more or less when they reveal similar factor endowments. The data we use have been provided by Gary Saxonhouse (1989) and measure four relative factor endowments in 1980 for a subsample of 36 countries: the ratios of capital over labor, education over labor, arable land over labor and oil over labor. These data are normalized to one for Denmark. We actually use the absolute values of the endowment differences between trading partners, and use levels rather than logs because of their small size. The results of the extended model are illustrated in appendix 3.

We only find two very significant coefficients (with t-values larger than two) which are both in the sample for 1980. It is possible, that endowments since 1980 have changed significantly and that therefore most coefficients in 1985 and

1990 are not significant. It appears that trade in 1980 was larger when differences in capital over labor endowments were small. That confirms our insights from empirical observations, showing that industrialized countries today conduct more than two-thirds of their trade as intra-industry trade, and that intra-industry trade is mainly conducted among similar industrialized economies.

Moreover, our results show a large and positive coefficient for differences in human capital (education over labor) in 1980, which remains positive for our samples in 1985 and 1990. That result may indicate that differences in human and not physical capital are most important in determining trade, and that countries with very different relative endowments of human capital trade significantly more. One more speculative hypothesis to explain the declining absolute values of coefficients both for physical and human capital during the 1980s is the emergence of multinational firms, which used FDI (physical capital) to employ foreign labor (human capital), which according to conventional trade theory makes relative endowments more similar.

The coefficients for relative land and relative oil endowments are nearly always positive, but not very significant. Interesting is also the change of coefficients for the three trading areas in our extended model: there is a clear tendency for the coefficient of East Asian countries to decline during the 1980s, showing that these countries have become more integrated into the world economy. Moreover, the coefficient for the European Community nearly doubles between 1980 and 1985 and remains at a constant level in 1990, indicating that in 1990 countries in the European Community on average traded 80% more with each other than with non-members.

FDI and PFI Data

Finally, we use the previous regression and add another set of independent variables, and distinguish four categories: *foreign direct investment* (FDI) as defined above is measured as net flows (two year averages over GNP) and stocks (sum of depreciated net inflows over GNP), and *portfolio investment* (PFI) is measured in the same categories of net flows and stocks.

Looking first at the sample for total trade (appendix 3c), we recognize three main results: First, net FDI inflows can either be substitutes (as in 1980) or complements (as in 1985) of international trade, but these effects are limited to the short term. Second, FDI stocks appear to have always a negative effect on international trade, which suggests that FDI inflows may during the initial first two years stimulate trade (flow effect), whereas they afterwards appear to be substitutes and hence depress international trade (stock effect). Third, the effects of FDI and PFI stocks appear to be very similar, suggesting that both FDI and PFI may be attracted by the same policies, and that the distinction between them is less obvious than revealed by the definitions. In fact, the coefficient of the FDI stock in 1980 appears to be more significant than all others, which suggests that PFI in 1980 had a similar effect as FDI in subsequent years (when accidentally a lot of Japanese PFI was reclassified as FDI).

Looking at the sample for exports and imports (appendices 3a and 3b), these three main results are confirmed: The coefficients of FDI and PFI stocks on trade are negative (with one exception of FDI stocks on imports in 1980); the effects of PFI stocks are always significant; and in the short term, FDI inflows may increase trade and indeed also alter the trade balance. In 1985, net FDI inflows stimulated both exports and imports, whereas in 1990, net FDI inflows (and also net PFI inflows) reduced exports and increased imports, thereby deteriorating the trade balance of countries receiving net FDI inflows with the opposite effects for countries with net FDI outflows.

The gravity model has given a clear answer to our question on what cumulative effect net FDI inflows have on trade -- they are clearly substitutes. On the other hand, the gravity model is not able to illustrate why and how that effect is realized. Therefore, we need complement our analysis with a section on macroeconomic considerations, illustrating the likely composition of this cumulative effect for three country examples. Before turning to these case studies, we should first address some pitfalls of the gravity model:

6. PITFALLS OF THE GRAVITY MODEL

Although our gravity model produces values of adjusted R-squared around 0.85, relatively high compared to previous studies, it poses many serious econometric problems. None of those problems however is unique to this particular gravity model, they nearly all apply to gravity models which have been used in previous studies. In fact, we tried to take a setup as similar as possible to previous studies (eg. Frankel and Wei, 1993), in order to reveal the differences from introducing factor endowments and FDI as new independent variables.

First, the functional log-linear form was chosen in order to reduce the weight of extreme or very large observations and because economic theory suggests a multiplicative relationship. However, we need to address a problem with many zero or close to zero trade flows, which are not allowed as arguments for a log function. We could estimate a Tobit maximum-likelihood model, another option would be to eliminate these values by setting them N/A, and we decided to take the latter approach, since it is more common in the literature. Our results would not change significantly if we had substituted a small positive value for all zero trade flows and then had corrected for heteroscedasticity (eg. White, 1980). Moreover, it is not obvious that all series are stationary, especially nominal trade and GNP values may have a common trend. However, all other variables (dummies, endowments, FDI) refer to levels and not changes in trade, so that taking the first differences would not improve our specification.

Second, we have to deal with multicollinearity and left-out variable bias at the same time: by leaving out variables of relative prices (such as the exchange rate), we certainly create some left-out variable bias, especially when estimating levels of imports and exports. On the other hand, we obtain some very unstable coefficients which suggest that there might be some degree of multicollinearity, for instance between GNP and GNP/capita variables, between the adjacency and regional trading block dummies, and also between FDI flows and GNP (through the indirect effect via higher investment, FDI inflows and GNP growth may be positively correlated).

Third, we may have a biased sample of observations, which also changes over time. Because some bilateral trade data are not available or zero and some FDI data are not reported, these observations are excluded from our sample which by definition introduces a bias. Once these data become available in later years, this bias is reduced and coefficients may change significantly. Also, some classifications for data may change over time (such as Japanese PFI during the 1980s or the membership in the European Community during the 1980s) so that structural changes in the model make previous coefficients unreliable.

All three discussed issues to some extent explain the inherent structural instability of the gravity model. When we test for the stability of coefficients in our three samples 1980, 1985, and 1990, we strongly reject the hypothesis that the four coefficients $\alpha 1$ through $\alpha 4$ remained stable, suggesting that even the impact of the main determinants of trade (GNP and population) change over time. Even the hypothesis that $\alpha 6$ is stable must be rejected, which says that neighboring countries change their tendency to trade with each other over time (for instance in appendix 3a, where the coefficient strongly increases in 1985). Moreover, we would expect that trade policies change the impact of the regional trading area dummies ($\alpha 8$) and that economic policies may change the impact of FDI on trade. Therefore, nearly all our coefficients are expected to change across time.

That criticism does not invalidate the findings of the gravity model, but it adds a substantial grain of caution to its interpretation. The gravity model very well explains historical trade flows as a function of many independent variables. However, the gravity model is absolutely inappropriate for predicting any future trade flows or for predicting any change in future trade flows caused by a change in a certain policy. That inability of the gravity model to predict future trade can be illustrated with two examples:

Trade between Spain and France is an observation above the mean in our sample. As revealed in table 2, the gravity model in 1985 and in 1990 explains actual bilateral trade between Spain and France very well, with deviations of only +5% and -1%. However, when we use the coefficients of the 1985 model with real 1990 data to predict 1990 trade, our prediction is far exaggerated with a deviation of 150%. In our second example, trade between Poland and Germany is an observation below the mean in our sample, which is expected to be rather different from average observations because of the different regimes. Still, our gravity model in 1985 and 1990 explains actual bilateral trade between Poland and Germany rather well, but when we calculate a prediction of 1990 trade based on the 1985 model, our estimate again is more than 40% off. Not surprisingly, most of this prediction error comes from huge changes in the constant, and in the case of Spanish-French trade also from changes of GNP coefficients.

Surprisingly, many previous studies which employed the gravity model not even report the constant in their regressions. In our example, the constant with an average value around 2 often explains more than 20% of total trade with a mean value of 3 billion dollars [exp(8)]. Moreover, changes in constants over time are often so dramatic, that they nearly explain the entire difference which occurs in trade flows over time, but which are usually attributed to a change in independent variables. Resuming the insights from our critical evaluation of the gravity model, it is important to recall again what Deardorff (1984) said: the gravity model tells us what is going on, but it doesn't tell us why. We might add, the gravity model tells us what happened in the past, but it should never be used for any future prediction. This somber result implies for our objective to study the impact of FDI on trade, that we can still conclude that in the past, FDI inflows have substituted international trade, but that we cannot use these results to make any future predictions, for instance on how much trade is going to be reduced by an expected volume of FDI inflows.

Table 2: Robustness of the Gravity Model

	Trade (mill. USD) Spain - France	**Trade (mill. USD) Poland - Germany**
1985 actual	7117	1954
1985 model	7475	2125
model deviation	+ 5 %	+ 9 %
1990 actual	25044	6639
1990 model	24884	5010
model deviation	-1%	-25%
	Prediction error using 1985 model for 1990 data	
1990 prediction	62068	9293
prediction error	+ 148 %	+ 40 %
	Sources of prediction error	
Change in Constant (1)	+ 167 %	+ 43 %
GNP and capita coefficients (4)	- 19 %	+ 4 %
Dummy coefficients (6)	- 26 %	- 8 %
Endowment coefficients (4)	- 8 %	+ 0 %
Investment coefficients (4)	+ 34 %	+ 1 %

Notes: Trade is the sum of exports plus imports (from UN data).
All variables in logs have been calculated in real levels at 1985 prices.
Spain's model includes a dummy of one for membership in the EC in 1990.
Poland's model includes a dummy of one for adjacency to Germany in 1990.

7. MACROECONOMIC CONSIDERATIONS

So far, our empirical estimations have shown that international trade and foreign direct investment appear to be negatively correlated. Our regressions also indicate that some time lag is present and that the trade balance might change. However, the gravity model did not reveal how these effects actually take place. Therefore we need to look at some country-studies as examples. Obviously, the selection of the sample is difficult, since we intend to illustrate the effects in a few typical cases. On the other hand, there are some exceptional cases, where the opposite effects occur, as for instance in the United Kingdom in 1989, where FDI outflows occurred together with a trade deficit. We screen the initial sample of countries by requiring that net FDI inflows in 1989 and 1990 were larger than 2% of GNP and that those inflows were larger than half of the country's FDI stock. Obviously, these criteria select countries with significant FDI inflows, which occurred in relative recent years, and they lead to a selection of six out of initially 63 countries in our sample, namely Spain, Portugal, Mexico, Malaysia, Philippines, and Thailand. We then select the three larger countries Spain, Mexico, and Thailand for our illustration.

Looking at these three examples, we observe a boom in FDI inflows in Spain since 1987, in Thailand since 1988, and in Mexico since 1989. As table 3 indicates, yearly capital inflows (which include FDI as one principal component) in Spain accounted for between 3% and 4% of GNP, whereas they ranged up to 7% of GNP in Mexico and up to 12% of GNP in Thailand. In all three cases, we also observed a subsequent deterioration of the current account, which was mainly reflected in a deteriorating trade balance. Current account deficits have reached 3.7% in Spain, 7.1% in Mexico, and 8.1% in Thailand. Moreover, in all three cases, private investment increased substantially, by 2.5% in Mexico, 4.2% in Spain, and 12.1% in Thailand, which contributed to a sustained increase in GDP over during the period of FDI inflows.

Patterns of capital inflows in these three countries were similar: inflows were mainly directed towards the private sector, portfolio investment was substantial in Spain and Mexico, and foreign direct investment accounted for about 20% of total capital inflows. It would however be a mistake to assume that all these inflows were rooted in common causes and have produced common effects, but there certainly have been some similarities. As a recent study has shown (Schadler, 1993), capital inflows were in general highly beneficial to the recipient country when they were motivated by improvements in financial stability and structural policies, but they had more destabilizing effects, when they reflected only temporary developments.

Table 3: Capital Inflows and Their Impact: Mexico/Spain/Thailand

(all in % of GNP)	Year 0	Year 1	Year 2	Year 3	Year 4
Mexico 1989					
Capital Inflows	-0.2	2.4	4.6	7.4	7.6
Real GDP(Δ%)	-0.3	3.3	4.4	3.6	2.6
Savings	18.9	18.6	18.6	16.6	15.0
Public	3.8	3.2	7.4	6.6	7.3
Private	15.1	15.5	11.2	10.0	7.7
Investment	19.4	21.6	21.8	21.3	22.0
Public	5.2	4.9	4.9	4.5	4.1
Private	14.2	16.7	16.9	16.8	17.9
Current Account	-0.5	-3.0	-3.2	-4.7	-7.1
Spain 1987					
Capital Inflows	-1.1	3.8	2.7	3.8	3.1
Real GDP(Δ%)	2.6	5.6	5.2	4.8	3.6
Savings	21.1	21.5	22.4	21.8	21.9
Public	-0.9	1.7	1.8	2.9	1.9
Private	22.0	19.8	20.6	18.9	20.0
Investment	19.6	21.5	23.7	25.1	25.5
Public	3.3	3.4	3.8	4.4	4.9
Private	16.3	18.1	19.9	20.7	20.6
Current Account	1.5	-0.1	-1.1	-3.2	-3.7
Thailand 1988					
Capital Inflows	3.3	5.2	9.7	11.4	12.6
Real GDP(Δ%)	5.5	13.2	12.0	10.0	8.2
Savings	22.2	26.1	27.9	29.3	30.1
Public	4.5	9.0	9.9	11.6	11.7
Private	17.7	17.1	18.0	17.4	18.6
Investment	23.5	28.8	31.5	38.3	38.2
Public	7.6	5.2	5.2	6.9	8.5
Private	15.9	23.6	26.3	31.0	29.8
Current Account	-1.3	-2.5	-3.4	-8.9	-8.1

Source: Schadler et. al. (1993) extracts from tables 1 and 7.

The causes of capital inflows have been rooted in external and especially in domestic factors. On the one hand, if domestic policies improved the potential productivity or reduced the public sector deficits, the capital inflows were relatively sustainable and often led to higher growth and investment. On the other hand, if a tightening of domestic credit policies attracted capital inflows, their impact was mainly to increase official reserves without any significant impact on investment and growth. It appears that FDI inflows may have had some indirect impact on trade, which has been complementary, because increasing growth, investment, and GDP usually lead to higher trade. The magnitude of this *indirect effect* across countries, however, has varied widely. It appears that Thailand was at the better end of the spectrum, where sustained fiscal consolidation and changes in regional investment patterns were main causes, whereas in Spain and Mexico, investment increased by much less, and interest rates remained relatively high.

The effects of capital inflows were also similar: Inflows usually financed a higher share of consumption, they weakened monetary control and tended to push up inflation, they rapidly led to a real appreciation of currencies in Spain (by 25%) and in Mexico (by 20%), which deteriorated the current account balance. Normally, current account deficits are reflected as increases in investment, but especially in Mexico they also revealed a drop in private savings. If the inflows indeed improved productivity and competitiveness, these effects were less signs of overheating than equilibrating adjustments, as in the case of

Thailand. If however, external events or credit policies caused capital inflows, these effects proved to be more destabilizing. Hence it appears that also an *exchange rate effect* has been at work, which to a different degree across countries has led to an appreciation of the currency and a worsening of the trade balance. In fact, all three countries experienced a large deterioration of their trade balance, which to a different degree may be attributed to exchange rate movements. However, this statement is value-neutral, since even a trade deficit may be desirable in certain circumstances.

There might be some parallel between the Dutch disease and the potential FDI disease: in the case of the Dutch disease, higher export receipts lead to higher consumption, a real appreciation of the exchange rate, and problems in implementing structural reforms. In the worst case of FDI inflows, they also increase consumption instead of investment, they push up the real exchange rate, deteriorate the trade balance and hinder structural reforms. In both cases, a reversal of previous capital inflows creates substantial problems, since the incurred additional expenditure (higher consumption or trade deficits) can no longer be sustained and relative prices need to shift back.

We find in our three case studies that the composition of the effect of FDI inflows on trade can widely vary and that it may include three channels: a direct effect, usually leading to trade substitution (relatively strong in Thailand); an indirect effect via investment and GNP growth, usually leading to an increase in trade (positive in Thailand, but actually negative in Mexico); and an exchange rate effect, usually leading to a deteriorating trade balance (relatively strong in Spain). However, while this small sample of three countries illustrates that the cumulative effect of FDI inflows on trade may be realized through three channels, it may not be representative and further research is needed to study possible other channels more in detail and to quantify more precisely the magnitude of the three effects we have identified.

8. CONCLUSIONS

FDI has been a positive twin of trade since both have been catalysts in integrating the global economy. It appears that the substantial increase of international trade during the last four decades was based on expanding intra-industry trade of manufactured products, while the rapid expansion of FDI during the 1980s indicated a shift towards the service sector, where FDI may be more effective than trade. Some theoretical studies characterized FDI as the negative twin of trade, since trade flows have been substituted by foreign investment flows, especially when they are factor-oriented. The theory of multinational firms, however, suggests that four categories exist to classify the twin: two positive ones (trade promoting and trade complementing) and two negative ones (trade substitution and trade diversion).

We addressed several problems in measuring foreign direct investment, distinguished between bilateral and multilateral effects, net and gross FDI, between FDI flows and stocks, and between FDI and PFI. We also made some strong symmetry assumptions, and focused our analysis on the cumulative effects of FDI inflows on trade. A gravity model has illustrated that for an average country, FDI stocks have a negative impact on trade, and that FDI flows may alter the trade balance. Then we addressed some serious concerns about the structural stability of the gravity model and concluded that it should not be used to interpret the effects or to make any future predictions. We finally complemented our analysis with some macroeconomic considerations derived from a limited case study of three countries, where FDI inflows led in all cases to a deteriorating trade balance, but where the combination of three effects we identified were very different: a direct effect of FDI inflows usually substitutes for trade; an indirect effect of FDI usually increases investment and complements trade; and an exchange rate effect usually deteriorates the trade balance.

These insights suggest that there is ample room for future research on the effects of FDI, especially on productivity, growth and trade. Moreover, the three channels we identified need some further qualification. Finally, the so much praised gravity model revealed serious shortcomings which suggest that some rethinking on its use is needed.

9. REFERENCES

Anderson, James E. (1979). "A Theoretical Foundation for the Gravity Equation". *American Economic Review.* 69: 106-116.

Ariff, M. (1989). "TRIMs A North-South Divide or a Non-Issue?". *World Economy.*

Baldwin, Richard. (1989). "The Growth Effects of 1992". *Economic Policy.* 9: 247-281.

Bergstrand, Jeffrey H. (1985). "The Gravity Equation in International Trade: some Microeconomic Foundations and Empirical Evidence". *Review of Economics and Statistics.* 67: 474-481.

Bergstrand, Jeffrey H. (1989). "The Generalized Gravity Equation, Monopolistic Competition,and the Factor-Proportions Theory in International Trade". *Review of Economics and Statistics.* 71: 143-153.

Casson, M. (1987). *"The Firm and the Market: Studies on Multinational Enterprises and the Scope of the Firm".* Basil Blackwell: Oxford.

Deardorff, Alan V. (1984). "Testing Trade Theories and Predicting Trade Flows". in: *"Handbook of International Economics".* Chapter 10. edited by R.W Jones and P.B. Kenen. Elsevier: Amsterdam.

Dixit, L. and J. Stiglitz. (1977). "Monopolistic Competition and Optimum Product Diversity". *American Economic Review.* 67: 297-308.

Dunning, J.H. (1958). *"American Investment in British Manufacturing Industry".* Allen & Unwin: London.

Dunning, J.H. (1977). "Trade, Location of Economic Activity and MNE: A Search for an Eclectic Approach. in: *"The International Allocation of Economic Activity"*. edited by B.Ohlin et. al. Macmillan: London.

Dunning, J.H. (1981). "Explaining the International Direct Investment Position of Countries: Towards a Dynamic or Developmental Approach". *Weltwirtschaftliches Archiv*. 117: 30-64.

Economist. (1990). "The Myth of Economic Sovereignty". 23. June 1990 p.67.

Ethier, Wilfred J. (1982). "National and International Returns to Scale in the Modern Theory of International Trade". *American Economic Review*. 72: 389-405.

Ethier, Wilfred J. (1986). "The Multinational Firm". *Quarterly Journal of Economics*. 101: 805-833.

Ethier, Wilfred J. and H. Horn. (1991). "Services in International Trade". in: *"international Trade and Trade Policy"*. pp. 223-244. edited by H. Helpman and A. Razin. MIT Press: Cambridge, Massachusetts.

Ethier, Wilfred J. (1992). "Multinational Firms in the Theory of International Trade". mimeo. Department of Economics. University of Pennsylvania.

Frankel, Jeffrey A. and Shang-Jin Wei. (1993). "Emerging Currency Blocks". Working Paper No. C93-026. Center for International and Development Economics Research. University of California at Berkeley.

Frankel, Jeffrey A., and Ernesto Stein, and Shang-Jin Wei. (1993). "Continental Trading Blocks: are they natural, or super-natural ?". NBER Working Paper No. 4588. Cambridge, Massachusetts.

Fratzscher, Oliver. (1994). "European Integration: Lessons from the South and Prospects for the East". in Schipke and Taylor (eds.): "*The Economics of Transformation: Theory and Practice in the New Market Economies*". Springer: New York. 191-232.

Graham, Edward and Paul Krugman. (1991). *"Direct Foreign Investment in the United States"*. second edition. Institute for International Economics: Washington, DC.

Havrylyshyn, Oleh and Lant Pritchett (1991). "European Trade Patterns after the Transition". PRE Working Paper No. 748. The World Bank. Washington, DC.

Helpman, Elhanan. (1984). "A Simple Theory of International Trade with Multinational Corporations". *Journal of Political Economy*. 92: 451-471.

Helpman, Elhanan and Paul R. Krugman. (1985). *"Market Structure and Foreign Trade"*. MIT Press: Cambridge, Massachusetts.

Hymer, S.H. (1976). *"The International Operations of National Firms: A Study of Direct Investment"*. MIT Press: Cambridge, Massachusetts.

International Monetary Fund (1977). *"Balance of Payments Manual"*. fourth edition. Washington, DC.

International Monetary Fund (1992). "Recent Trends in FDI for the Developing World". *Finance & Development*. March 1992. 29(1): 50-52.

International Monetary Fund (1994). *"Direction of Trade Statistics"*. Washington DC.

International Monetary Fund (1994). "*International Financial Statistics*". Washington DC.

Julius, DeAnne. (1990). "*Global Companies and Public Policy: The Growing Challenge of Foreign Direct Investment.*" Chatham House Paper: London.

Julius, DeAnne. (1991). "Foreign Direct Investment: The Neglected Twin of Trade". *Group of Thirty:* Washington, DC.

Jungnickel, Rolf. (1993). "Recent Trends in Foreign Direct Investment". *Intereconomics:* 118-125.

Kindleberger, C.P. (1969). "*American Business Abroad*". Yale University Press: New Haven.

Krugman, Paul R. (1979). "Increasing Returns, Monopolistic Competition and International Trade". *Journal of International Economics.* 9: 469-479.

Krugman, Paul R. (1980). "Scale Economies, Product Differentiation, and the Pattern of Trade". *American Economic Review.* 70: 950-959.

Lancaster, K. (1980). "Intra-Industry Trade under Perfect Monopolistic Competition". *Journal of International Economics.* 10: 151-176.

Leamer, Edward E. (1992). "Testing Trade Theory". NBER Working Paper No. 3958. Cambridge, Massachusetts.

Leontief, Wassily. (1953). "*Studies in the Structure of the American Economy: Theoretical and Empirical Explorations in Input-Output Analysis*". Oxford University Press: New York.

Linneman, H. (1966). *"An Empirical Study of International Trade Flows"*. North Holland: Amsterdam.

Markusen, J.R. (1984). "Multinationals, Multi-Plant Economies, and the Gains from Trade". *Journal of International Economics.* 16: 205-226.

Rugman, Alan M. (1980). "Internalization as a General Theory of Foreign Direct Investment: A Re-Appraisal of the Literature". *Weltwirtschaftliches Archiv.* 116: 365-379.

Saxonhouse, Gary. (1989). "Differentiated Products, Economies of Scale, and Access to the Japanese Market". in: *"Trade Policies for International Competitiveness"*. edited by R. Feenstra. 145-174. University of Chicago Press: Chicago.

Schadler, Susan et. al. (1993). "Recent Experiences with Surges in Capital Inflows". Occasional Paper No. 108. International Monetary Fund. Washington, DC.

UNCTC (1992). *"World Investment Report 1992"*. New York.

Wang, Zhen Kun and Alan Winters (1991). "Eastern Europe's Trading Potential", CEPR Discussion Paper No. 610. London.

White, Halbert. (1980). "A Heteroscedasticity-consistent Covariant Matrix Estimator and A Direct Test for Heteroskedasticity". *Econometrica:* 817-838.

10. Appendix 1: FDI Effects on Trade in a Three-Country-World

<I.> Initial Equilibrium

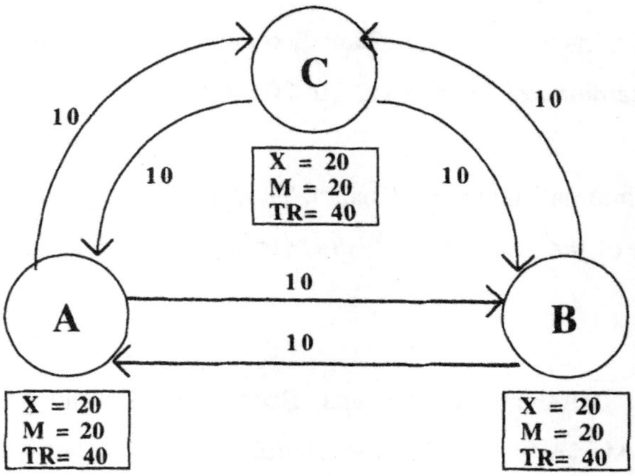

<II.> FDI-Flows of 10 from A to B:

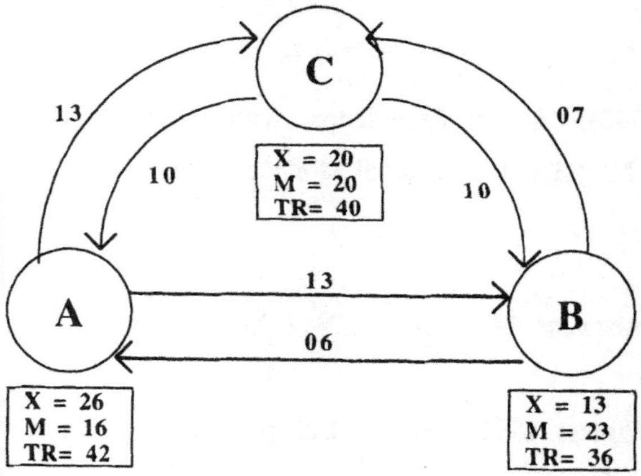

Country A:	Capital Account: -10 (FDI outflow) Current Account: +10 (Trade surplus) Exchange Rate depreciated NET FDI = -10 => Δ Trade = +2
Country B:	Capital Account: +10 (FDI inflow) Current Account: -10 (Trade deficit) Exchange Rate appreciated NET FDI = +10 => Δ Trade = -4
Country C:	capital and current account balanced trade surplus with B, trade deficit with A NET FDI = 0 => Δ Trade = 0
World:	Total NET FDI = +10 => Δ Total Trade = -2

11. Appendix 2a: Gravity Model of International Trade (Basic Model) - Exports:

Dependent: # Obs.: Adjusted R^2: S.E.E.: D.W.:	EXPORTS-1980 1953 0.6918 1.23 1.53		EXPORTS-1985 1953 0.6936 1.20 1.43		EXPORTS-1990 1953 0.7033 1.24 1.39	
Independent:	**Coefficient**	**T-Statistic**	**Coefficient**	**T-Statistic**	**Coefficient**	**T-Statistic**
CONSTANT	1.8279	4.4041	2.5623	6.3055	1.5818	3.8059
GNP of Country i	0.8431	33.5075	0.7760	31.3051	0.7694	31.1321
GNP of Country j	0.7159	26.2128	0.7497	28.3436	0.7582	29.7099
GNP/capita of Country i	0.3784	10.2837	0.3268	8.8030	0.2314	7.2181
DISTANCE between ports (i,j)	-0.6152	-13.3133	-0.6605	-14.3381	-0.5787	-12.5408
ADJACENCY (i,j) (Dummy)	0.4746	2.5206	0.7097	3.6956	0.7185	3.8784
SAME LANGUAGE (i,j) (Dummy)	0.4545	4.1362	0.3848	3.3756	0.4643	4.1984
(i,j) inside EUROPE (Dummy)	0.3306	1.7734	0.6116	3.3544	0.8245	4.3652
(i,j) inside WEST.HEM. (Dummy)	0.4891	2.9570	0.1556	0.8758	0.3451	2.0718
(i,j) inside EAST ASIA (Dummy)	2.0438	10.0907	1.4655	7.4934	2.3797	11.8126

11. Appendix 2b: Gravity Model of International Trade (Basic Model) - Imports:

Dependent:	**IMPORTS-1980**		**IMPORTS-1985**		**IMPORTS-1990**	
# Obs.:	**1953**		**1953**		**1953**	
Adjusted R^2:	**0.6513**		**0.6669**		**0.6817**	
S.E.E.:	**1.29**		**1.31**		**1.27**	
D.W.:	**1.57**		**1.47**		**1.37**	
Independent:	**Coefficient**	**T-Statistic**	**Coefficient**	**T-Statistic**	**Coefficient**	**T-Statistic**
CONSTANT	1.1216	2.5794	3.1368	7.1103	1.5155	3.5002
GNP of Country i	0.8358	37.4151	0.8131	36.1109	0.7958	38.1494
GNP of Country j	0.6597	22.6995	0.6984	23.7481	0.6932	24.2755
GNP/capita of Country j	0.4066	14.1393	0.4114	13.6830	0.3298	12.2272
DISTANCE between ports (i,j)	-0.4566	-9.3376	-0.7159	-14.1754	-0.5326	-10.9676
ADJACENCY (i,j) (Dummy)	0.7848	4.0608	0.7132	3.5057	0.6836	3.5465
SAME LANGUAGE (i,j) (Dummy)	0.4939	4.3943	0.4511	3.8172	0.5437	4.7028
(i,j) inside EUROPE (Dummy)	0.3087	1.5672	0.4895	2.4515	0.4599	2.3491
(i,j) inside WEST.HEM. (Dummy)	0.0770	0.4561	0.1420	0.7819	0.1524	0.8706
(i,j) inside EAST ASIA (Dummy)	1.8773	9.0150	1.5239	7.1358	2.1457	10.3871

11. Appendix 2c: Gravity Model of International Trade (Basic Model) - Trade:

Dependent:	**TRADE-1980**		**TRADE-1985**		**TRADE-1990**	
# Obs.:	**1953**		**1953**		**1953**	
Adjusted R^2:	**0.7165**		**0.7444**		**0.7470**	
S.E.E.:	**1.06**		**1.00**		**1.00**	
D.W.:	**1.47**		**1.31**		**1.29**	
Independent:	**Coefficient**	**T-Statistic**	**Coefficient**	**T-Statistic**	**Coefficient**	**T-Statistic**
CONSTANT	2.0161	5.4929	3.3562	9.6330	2.1018	6.0298
GNP of Country i	0.7923	34.5959	0.7525	33.9676	0.7528	34.7943
GNP of Country j	0.6680	26.9186	0.7156	29.9241	0.6621	28.6851
GNP/capita of Country i	0.1732	5.1811	0.1439	4.2584	0.0703	2.4236
GNP/capita of Country j	0.3008	12.2091	0.2840	11.6381	0.2503	11.4444
DISTANCE between ports (i,j)	-0.4588	-11.1107	-0.6096	-15.2278	-0.4586	-11.7471
ADJACENCY (i,j) (Dummy)	0.6743	4.1356	0.6559	4.0243	0.6557	4.2351
SAME LANGUAGE (i,j) (Dummy)	0.4297	4.4242	0.4582	4.6393	0.5175	5.4726
(i,j) inside EUROPE (Dummy)	0.1821	1.1235	0.4297	2.8008	0.6149	3.9627
(i,j) inside WESTERN (Dummy)	0.2121	1.4809	0.0970	0.6497	0.1764	1.2499
(i,j) inside EAST ASIA (Dummy)	1.9697	11.1881	1.4712	8.8541	2.1797	13.1440

12. Appendix 3a: Gravity Model of International Trade (Ext. Model) - Exports:

Dependent:	EXPORTS-1980		EXPORTS-1985		EXPORTS-1990	
# Obs.:	1875		1875		1862	
Adjusted R^2:	0.8093		0.7887		0.8276	
S.E.E.:	0.98		1.02		0.95	
D.W.:	1.54		1.48		1.56	
Independent:	**Coefficient**	**T-Statistic**	**Coefficient**	**T-Statistic**	**Coefficient**	**T-Statistic**
CONSTANT	0.7830	1.2233	1.4734	2.3549	0.1296	0.1972
GNP of Country i	0.7786	15.3072	0.6729	12.9167	0.7268	16.7909
GNP of Country j	0.7896	20.5395	0.7855	20.3851	0.8247	23.1544
GNP/capita of Country i	0.6192	4.6803	0.6850	4.5203	0.6340	3.9561
DISTANCE between ports (i,j)	-0.5276	-8.2114	-0.5576	-8.3102	-0.5290	-8.5067
ADJACENCY (i,j) (Dummy)	0.5825	2.1353	0.8889	3.1401	0.5271	1.9729
SAME LANGUAGE (i,j) (Dummy)	0.6464	3.5225	0.2890	1.5402	0.8145	4.4319
(i,j) inside EUROPE (Dummy)	0.3939	1.9141	0.7547	3.5555	0.6029	3.0348
(i,j) inside WEST.HEM. (Dummy)	0.4653	1.2038	-0.4980	-1.2471	-0.2977	-0.7428
(i,j) inside EAST ASIA (Dummy)	1.5193	3.6524	1.2349	2.8543	0.9351	2.3103
CAPITAL/L Endowment D	-0.5002	-3.1819	-0.1959	-1.2262	-0.2091	-1.3676
EDUCATION/L Endowment D	0.7723	3.4202	0.3694	1.5731	0.2843	1.2920
ARABLE LAND/L Endowment D	0.0289	0.8355	0.0329	0.9196	0.0229	0.6632
OIL/L Endowment D	-0.0054	-0.6714	0.0009	0.1134	0.0135	1.7948
FDI FLOWS (last 2 years/GNP)	1.6617	0.2252	12.5439	2.8495	-6.0583	-2.0874
FDI STOCK (depr sum/GNP)	-15.7336	-1.9144	-7.0981	-3.8455	-0.0041	-0.0015
PFI FLOWS (last 2 years/GNP)	-1.3271	-0.4376	-4.4018	-4.3584	-0.9847	-0.4329
PFI STOCK (depr sum/GNP)	-6.0948	-2.5969	-2.8070	-3.3594	-4.3989	-3.2225

12. Appendix 3b: Gravity Model of International Trade (Ext. Model) - Imports:

Dependent:	**IMPORTS-1980**		**IMPORTS-1985**		**IMPORTS-1990**	
# Obs.:	**1875**		**1875**		**1862**	
Adjusted R^2:	**0.7600**		**0.7860**		**0.7737**	
S.E.E.:	**1.13**		**1.06**		**1.15**	
D.W.:	**1.80**		**1.71**		**1.55**	
Independent:	**Coefficient**	**T-Statistic**	**Coefficient**	**T-Statistic**	**Coefficient**	**T-Statistic**
CONSTANT	0.2220	0.3101	2.4784	3.8132	0.9174	1.2630
GNP of Country i	0.8199	15.1755	0.7124	16.5902	0.7470	15.5555
GNP of Country j	0.6900	14.7192	0.7464	17.2055	0.7740	16.4044
GNP/capita of Country j	0.3472	7.5696	0.3145	7.2289	0.2101	4.7528
DISTANCE between ports (i,j)	-0.3545	-4.6434	-0.5514	-7.6244	-0.4402	-5.5837
ADJACENCY (i,j) (Dummy)	0.9729	3.0967	0.7258	2.4514	0.6394	1.9700
SAME LANGUAGE (i,j) (Dummy)	0.8633	4.0165	0.6712	3.3599	1.0054	4.4313
(i,j) inside EUROPE (Dummy)	0.3914	1.6548	0.6178	2.8008	0.6075	2.5236
(i,j) inside WEST.HEM. (Dummy)	0.1386	0.3132	-0.2526	-0.6051	0.1992	0.4091
(i,j) inside EAST ASIA (Dummy)	1.6506	3.4300	1.1981	2.6345	1.1704	2.3692
CAPITAL/L Endowment D	-0.0589	-0.3366	-0.0320	-0.1894	0.1401	0.7589
EDUCATION/L Endowment D	0.3226	1.2364	-0.1892	-0.7526	-0.4314	-1.6114
ARABLE LAND/L Endowment D	0.0692	1.7623	0.0283	0.7578	0.0625	1.4810
OIL/L Endowment D	-0.0039	-0.4250	0.0014	0.1634	0.0140	1.5277
FDI FLOWS (last 2 years/GNP)	-31.6750	-3.7775	3.8968	0.9304	5.8386	1.6762
FDI STOCK (depr sum/GNP)	21.1715	2.2680	-8.5309	-4.4406	-11.0246	-3.2582
PFI FLOWS (last 2 years/GNP)	6.6082	1.8794	-2.3752	-2.2014	0.9715	0.3435
PFI STOCK (depr sum/GNP)	-10.0577	-3.6450	-4.9462	-5.5612	-6.9646	-4.0428

12. Appendix 3c: Gravity Model of International Trade (Ext. Model) - Trade:

Dependent:	TRADE-1980		TRADE-1985		TRADE-1990	
# Obs.:	1875		1875		1862	
Adjusted R^2:	0.8284		0.8451		0.8307	
S.E.E.:	0.87		0.81		0.88	
D.W.:	1.67		1.47		1.49	
Independent:	Coefficient	T-Statistic	Coefficient	T-Statistic	Coefficient	T-Statistic
CONSTANT	0.6636	1.1456	2.4383	4.7376	1.5726	2.3711
GNP of Country i	0.6815	14.7150	0.6287	14.8087	0.7029	16.9816
GNP of Country j	0.6907	19.0462	0.7534	22.5994	0.7443	20.4283
GNP/capita of Country i	0.5848	4.9521	0.3768	2.7484	0.1424	0.7739
GNP/capita of Country j	0.2849	8.0291	0.2202	6.6197	0.1704	5.0236
DISTANCE between ports (i,j)	-0.3299	-5.5685	-0.4719	-8.5037	-0.4091	-6.7689
ADJACENCY (i,j) (Dummy)	0.9496	3.9256	0.8520	3.7820	0.6120	2.4608
SAME LANGUAGE (i,j) (Dummy)	0.7542	4.5447	0.4694	3.0875	0.8724	5.0159
(i,j) inside EUROPE (Dummy)	0.3698	2.0292	0.6604	3.9188	0.6104	3.3091
(i,j) inside WESTERN (Dummy)	0.3585	1.0461	-0.3771	-1.1889	-0.0757	-0.2033
(i,j) inside EAST ASIA (Dummy)	1.8826	5.0664	1.4421	4.1718	1.1944	3.1580
CAPITAL/L Endowment D	-0.4196	-2.9889	-0.1000	-0.7643	-0.1015	-0.7024
EDUCATION/L Endowment D	0.5386	2.6533	0.0848	0.4389	0.1251	0.6020
ARABLE LAND/L Endowment D	0.0192	0.6233	0.0127	0.4465	0.0361	1.1146
OIL/L Endowment D	-0.0038	-0.5265	-0.0018	-0.2735	0.0107	1.5245
FDI FLOWS (last 2 years/GNP)	-10.0671	-1.5263	9.3338	2.5278	-1.2345	-0.4360
FDI STOCK (depr sum/GNP)	-0.9694	-0.1314	-8.6872	-5.5662	-4.3226	-1.6613
PFI FLOWS (last 2 years/GNP)	-0.0625	-0.0230	-2.7593	-3.3008	0.4554	0.2072
PFI STOCK (depr sum/GNP)	-8.1824	-3.8418	-4.8255	-7.0463	-5.4722	-4.1093

13. Appendix 3d: Gravity Model of International Trade - Notes:

- All variables are in logarithms, except dummies, endowments, and investments are in levels.
- Endowments are in absolute differences (D) between trading partners i and j.
- Trade Data have been provided by Shang-Jin Wei.
- Distance Data have been provided by Lant Pritchett.
- Endowment Data have been provided by Gray Saxonhouse.
- Investment Data are from International Monetary Fund, IFS.
- GNP Data are from International Monetary Fund, IFS and World Bank, World Tables 1992.

List of 63 Countries used in the Gravity Equation:

(WEST.HEM.)
Canada
United States
Argentina
Brazil
Chile
Colombia
Ecuador
Mexico
Peru
Venezuela
Bolivia
Paraguay
Uruguay

(EUROPE)
Belgium
Denmark
France
Germany
Greece
Ireland
Italy
Netherlands
Portugal
Spain
United Kingdom

(EFTA)
Austria
Finland
Norway
Sweden
Switzerland
Iceland

(EAST ASIA)
Japan
Indonesia
Taiwan
Hong Kong
Korea
Malaysia
Philippines
Singapore
Thailand
China

(OTHERS)
South Africa
Turkey
Yugoslavia
Israel
Algeria
Libya
Nigeria
Egypt
Morocco
Tunisia
Sudan
Ghana
Kenya
Ethiopia
Iran
Kuwait
Saudi Arabia
India
Pakistan
Hungary
Poland
Australia
New Zealand

GPSR Compliance

The European Union's (EU) General Product Safety Regulation (GPSR) is a set of rules that requires consumer products to be safe and our obligations to ensure this.

If you have any concerns about our products, you can contact us on ProductSafety@springernature.com

In case Publisher is established outside the EU, the EU authorized representative is:

Springer Nature Customer Service Center GmbH
Europaplatz 3
69115 Heidelberg, Germany

Batch number: 10725973

Printed by Printforce, the Netherlands